The Handy Guide for Your iPhone
iPhone XR

Matthew Stone

Table Of Contents

Introduction

The year 2018 was a fantastic year for iPhone lovers and enthusiasts, given the trifecta of devices that the tech giant released. Known for their high-end devices, Apple followed in the footsteps of iPhone XS and XS Max with the XR, a device dubbed as the cheapest iPhone device of the year. This sentiment alone is bound to get people excited about getting their hands on this device.

We must, however, address the fact that the term *cheapest* should not be misconstrued with substandard services. Even with the lowest cost offering of the iPhones released in the year, the iPhone XR still packs a punch, compared to most of the devices in the market in its price range. You still get the amazing, powerful experience you would expect from any iPhone device.

If you are buying the XR, you are looking forward to a fantastic device that has taken the smartphone market by storm – obviously! While the other devices retailed at $1,099 and $999, the XR hit the market at $749. For an average smartphone user, and we are talking Android devices here, $749 still sounds a bit pricey. For an avid iPhone user, $749 is quite a steal!

You can get the iPhone XR in the following storage capacities, and prices:

- 64 GB for $749

- 128 GB for $799

- 256 GB for $899

The iPhone XR runs on iOS 12. Public access to the iOS 12 was slated much earlier before the iPhone XR was, which means customers already have an experience of the new upgraded operating system. By the time you get your hands on the iPhone XR, you might expect a few updates, patches and bug fixes to the iOS already rolled out.

While the XR might look slightly different from the other iPhone devices released in the market this year, what runs under the hood is just as amazing as what you would expect from Apple. They outdid themselves on this one.

Want to have a device that stands out? iPhone XR comes in six different colors, blue, coral, yellow, red, white and black. The XS and XS Max, on the other hand, are only available in three colors each. Other than the six color options available, you can take things further, and choose to get an iPhone cover for your XR, which adds even more styling options. Regarding aesthetics, the XR is a beast.

While the XR beats the XS and XS Max on aesthetics, they beat it hands down on the camera and display features, which have been poised as their major selling points. Besides that, however, the XR, XS and XS Max are pretty much cut from the same cloth. If you are currently using an iPhone 8 or an older model, upgrading to the iPhone XR would be a brilliant idea.

Chapter 1: iPhone XR Processor

Let's start with the bionic chip. XR runs the same A12 chip that you will find in XS and XS Max. Other than the fact that it powers the higher end models of this device, what is so special about this chip? Of all the processors Apple has used over the years, the A12 bionic processor is their greatest introduction yet. The in-house system on a chip (SoC) processor combines multiple processing cores at insane energy levels, allowing you to command some intensive tasks.

For light work like browsing the internet and checking your emails, the A12 bionic processor makes quite a meal thanks to the high-efficiency cores. Six cores power this processor CPU, and an additional eight core neural engine that supports the machine learning systems built into the iPhone XR.

According to Apple, the A12 bionic chip is designed to power at least 5 trillion operations a second.

It is not easy to understand why this statistic means so much unless you compare it with the previous installment. At 7-nanometers, the A12 bionic chip processor is a breath of fresh air compared to the previous 10-nanometer A11 chip that could power through 600 billion operations a second. Given that the XR, XS and XS Max run the same A12 bionic chip, the XR is, therefore, just as compelling under the hood as the others.

Chapter 2: iPhone XR Battery

Something you will fancy about the iPhone XR is drawing comparisons with the XS and XS Max, especially since you are paying much less to get it.

Let's have a look at the battery. The XR features a 2,942 mAh battery. Of course, this comes nowhere close to the flagship iPhones with a battery capacity of more than 4,000 mAh. However, why is this important? Well, the XS only runs a 2,658 mAh battery. So, for a few bucks less, you are getting more juice out of the XR. The XS Max, however, features a 3,174 mAh battery.

The official battery specifications for the iPhone XR according to Apple are as follows:

- Up to 25 hours talk time on wireless

- Up to 15 hours on internet use

- Up to 16 hours video playback on wireless

- Up to 65 hours audio playback on wireless

Compared to the iPhone 8 Plus, you have around one and a half hours more battery life, which makes it a good idea for someone who is looking for an upgrade.

Also, a bonus, Apple also included wireless charging on the iPhone XR.

Chapter 3: iPhone XR Display

The iPhone XR display is one of the features that has got many people talking. Many people have by now experienced the OLED screens that are popular in the market and would have expected the iPhone XR to follow suit. However, Apple decided to go with an LCD screen.

The iPhone XR, instead of going the OLED way as has been witnessed in models like iPhone X and iPhone XS, was built with LCD screens. It is an interesting decision, given that LCD screens are considered a thing of the past. However, according to Apple, the LCD used in the iPhone XR is more of a futuristic approach.

Why would Apple go this way? It is important to note that Apple still stays true to the LCD screens as their standard display technology for their devices. Even with an LCD screen in the face of OLED competition, Apple still takes a win with the XR, given that they have designed a device that, for the very first time, has the entire front face of the camera covered. On the iPhone XR, it has been tagged the Liquid Retina display. What this means is that Apple has done away with the chin and forehead design that users have been accustomed to for a long time.

Perhaps the screen is not one of the most amazing features of the iPhone XR. While the other phones in its class come with amazing OLED displays, it only comes with an LCD screen. The 6.1 inches in your hands will perhaps make up for this if you fancy a gigantic screen. The thing with LCD screens is that they are not as bright as OLED screens. So, other than the massive screen in your hand, you should not expect the crisp, liquid clear clarity you will find in the XS and XS Max.

What makes this LCD screen different from archaic models? The screen on the iPhone XR, like the OLED screens, is rounded from one corner to the other. It features sub-pixel and masking skills, and an additional LED back-lighting. The backlight on the iPhone XR LCD screen helps to support lightning depression and also helps to make up for the lack of 3D Touch for Haptic Touch.

Concerning screen size, the iPhone XR is, in fact, the second largest device that Apple has released. It is sandwiched in size by the iPhone XS Max and the iPhone XS. The iPhone XR comes with 6.1 inches of screen size, which is a big deal compared to 5.8 inches that we have seen in the iPhone X and iPhone XS.

If you have been looking for an upgrade in screen size, the iPhone XR will make a good candidate. It is only second to the iPhone XS Max, which comes in at 6.5 inches. For many an iPhone user, 6.1 inches is an ideal size, given that people have been asking for a long time whether Apple would follow in the footsteps of the Android competitors and release widescreen phones.

The iPhone market is advancing in light of consumer demands, and a big screen is considered something most people are looking for. There are a number of users who still appreciate the smaller devices, like the iPhone SE. However, the fact remains that people are looking forward to bigger devices, and for a good reason.

In recent years, we have seen larger phones eat into the market share for tablets, killing smaller size tablets in the process. A big screen is, considered an appropriate device that cuts across cultural and gender divides, hence the 6.1 inches on the iPhone XR is a welcome move.

We must also appreciate the fact that phones are currently one of the key communications and computing devices for most people, and the move toward a bigger screen is about increasing creativity and productivity.

Building on the screen size, the iPhone XR shares a lot of advantages with the iPhone XS Max. One of these features is the Display Zoom, a feature that is designed to make the device more accessible. With the Display Zoom, it is easier to see things clearly on the large screen. Interactions are enhanced, and your touch capacity is also improved. This is also designed to help you navigate faster when using the iPhone XR, especially when you are going through lists with finer details.

A large screen is only as good as you can enjoy utility value from it. With the iPhone XR, you can enjoy reachability, accessing the top of your phone screen from the middle. The iPhone XR employs the X-style navigation system for gestures. It might take a while getting used to this, but when you do, you will be able to enjoy the Home button experience.

For all the good things that have been said about the iPhone XR, there is not much to look forward to about the resolution and density, unless this is your first experience with an iPhone. Those who have used iPhones over the years will notice the differences.

The iPhone XS and iPhone XS Max both feature impressive screen resolutions, at 2436 x1125 and 2688 x 1942 respectively, with 458 ppi. The iPhone XR, on the other hand, features a paltry 1792 x 828 resolution, with 326 ppi.

It might not feel right comparing an OLED screen with an LCD screen, especially when you look at the foundational design and build of the screens. They are two different technologies. When addressing the differences in terms of the advantages and disadvantages of LCD and OLED screens, the disparities are at best, relative. It would take a lot to put them side by side in a fair comparison.

A lot of people would feel an LCD screen is a step back, but this is not true. There are challenges that are faced by the OLED screens too, however advanced people believe they are. Some of the common challenges that you would experience when using an OLED screen include an off-axis color shift and black smearing. With an LCD screen, you do not have to worry about black smearing or off-axis color shift. That being said, however, LCD is simply not as alluring and desirable as an OLED screen. OLED screens offer an amazing deep black hue and a high contrast range that you would never experience in the LCD screen on the iPhone XR.

What Apple has done with the iPhone XR is to give the LCD a new lease of life, pushing it as far as they can. You can, however, not expect to get the HDR (high dynamic range) experience, but the color scheme and calibration in the iPhone XR is amazing. On this feature, the iPhone XR offers pretty much the same experience you would get in an iPhone XS.

The display on the iPhone XR is not 1080p. This does not mean you will not get an amazing experience with this device. However, unless you plan on using VR on your device where you should be getting 4K on either eye, the 326 ppi available with the iPhone XR is decent, especially for normal viewing distances.

For normal use, however, you should not notice any difference when using the iPhone XR. It is a fantastic device which promises to deliver an amazing user experience.

Chapter 4: Camera and Resolution

The camera is one of the key features a lot of people consider if they plan to buy an iPhone, and the iPhone XR is no different. The camera built into the iPhone XR is leveraged on the power of the A12 chip, delivering some fantastic capabilities.

You are getting a 7-megapixel selfie camera, which is the same specification used in the iPhone XS and iPhone XS Max. What you might not be able to enjoy, however, is the zoom feature. The picture quality is not as good as you would expect in an iPhone.

You have a 12-megapixel rear camera on the iPhone XR. All you can do with this camera is a digital zoom. The problem with cameras that are limited to digital zoom is that the quality can be grainy. This is a concern, especially when you compare the iPhone XR with iPhone XS and iPhone XS Max, which have a telephoto lens with optical zoom. The camera on the iPhone XR, however, gets saved by the A12 bionic chip. This powerful processor allows you to edit the depth of field in your photos after your shots.

The power behind the A12 bionic processor is responsible for the amazing graphics performance, real-time machine learning, and amazing photo processing capabilities that you get with the iPhone XR. This device also features an improved image signal processor and improved sensors. While it only has a 12 MP camera that has been a mainstay for many years, you can still enjoy detailed photos. With the Smart HDR function, you can improve your photos thanks to machine learning. Even though you only have one camera on the iPhone XR, you can still take decent photos in portrait mode.

The iPhone XR has a resolution of 1792 x 828 pixels, with a 326 PPI density. The iPhone XS, on the other hand, has a 2436 x 1125 resolution, and a 458 PPI. What this means is that with the iPhone XR, you can only enjoy watching videos up to 828p. This is good for most of the videos you can come across during your mobile experience. However, if you are looking to enjoy an unrivaled YouTube or Netflix experience on your iPhone XR, you might be slightly disappointed. You should, however, still be able to render most games on the iPhone without a hitch.

Chapter 5: The Power of iOS 12

One of the things you will love about the iPhone XR is iOS 12. This revamped upgrade gives you one of the best iPhone experiences to date. You are looking at an iPhone that performs faster than most, is delightful and more responsive. Everyone loves a responsive device. The iOS 12 has been dubbed one of the most advanced operating systems on mobile devices yet.

What makes it stand out?

Regarding performance, the iOS 12 is designed to help you speed things up. Everything you have been using your iPhone for in the past, you can now do the same, at insane speeds. Take swiping your camera, for example, whose response has been improved by 70%.

You are also looking at a 50% improvement in the keyboard display speed, and if you are using your iPhone under a heavy workload, you will be able to launch apps up to two times faster than before.

The performance enhancements are some of the reasons why you are going to enjoy using the iOS 12 on your iPhone XR. Other minor enhancements go towards giving you an overall amazing experience on the iPhone XR.

Fancy some FaceTime with friends and family members? You can now interact with up to 32 people at the same time. The audio and video enhancements on the iPhone XR powered by the iOS 12 make this a lot easier. In a group setting, if someone is speaking, their tile is enlarged, allowing you to stay focused on the conversation.

iOS 12.1.1

When Apple released iOS 12.1.1, one group of users who had a lot to look forward to was iPhone XR users. With the update, you can now enjoy some of the Haptic Feedback features that were not present previously. This adds functionality to the device, especially when you use a long press to get more out of your notifications.

The updates released thus far are small, but allow you to enjoy utmost utility out of your iPhone XR. It has not been a smooth sailing experience for everyone, however. Soon after the upgrade, there have been issues with some users experiencing trouble connecting to their cellular networks. It is not a widespread concern, because the frequency of reports to this problem is random.

Other users have also reported enjoying full cellular use on their iPhone XR devices with select apps, but not all the apps. What this alludes to is that the device can identify and pick up the connection to a cellular signal, but the operating system is struggling to manage the connection.

This update includes support for third-party navigation assistance apps instead of having to depend on Apple Maps all the time. You can look forward to using Google Maps, for example, in CarPlay for iOS 12. However, you must update to the current release. Google Maps is popular for accurate information in terms of traffic information, finding places, and alternative routes. The fact that you can enjoy it in the in-built display on your device is a plus.

Assuming that you started getting directions on your iPhone XR and then you got into your car, you simply need to connect to CarPlay and Google Maps will continue from where you left on the phone.

If you are planning your commute between your home and the workplace, Google Maps will provide you live updates on traffic so you can plan your route efficiently. You also get access to some of the favorite spots you frequent, which is a good way to remind you to pick up something you might have forgotten.

Another important feature that you will enjoy with the iOS 12.1.1 upgrade on your iPhone XR is dual SIM support. This is a feature that iPhones have barely taken seriously over the years. However, the update enables an eSIM that comes built into the iPhone XR, iPhone XS, and iPhone XS Max. Instead of getting a second physical SIM card, you can simply activate your cellular plan on a different network.

Chapter 6: Setting Up Your iPhone XR

Once you get your hands on your new iPhone XR, you are probably excited about firing it up and enjoying what it has to offer. Here are some features that will get you buzzing right away:

Face ID – allows you to confirm mobile payments and unlock your phone with ease, so setting this up right away will be a good idea.

Because the traditional physical home button no longer exists on the iPhone XR, you will want to learn how to do simple things like closing apps, taking screenshots, turning off the device and switching between the apps you are using.

Once you have the device out of the box, you can set it up in the following ways:

- As a new device, a fresh installation without restoring any old settings from previous phones.

- Restore old photos, music, apps and anything else from a cloud backup or a backup in your iTunes account.

- Restore data from an Android device.

iTunes Backup

Power on the device and select your country and language. Your iPhone XR will prompt you to either restore settings from a backup, move data from your old Android device, or to set up your iPhone XR as a new phone.

Choose "Restore from an iTunes backup."

Use the provided Lightning to USB cable that comes with your device and connect it to your computer. In case your MacBook only has USB Type C ports, you must buy the Lightning to USB Type C cable.

If iTunes does not open automatically, open it, you will be asked to allow the computer to access iPhone settings and information. Your iPhone will prompt you to accept whether you trust the connected computer.

On your iPhone, tap Trust, and on your computer, click Continue.

You will get a greeting message on the iPhone. Click Continue and Get Started.

Choose your iPhone on the list of devices that you can see on the left panel. Click on the iPhone summary tab. This tab should provide information on the type of device you are using, and useful information about the backups you have.

Select Restore Backup. In case you had saved backups for different devices, you can look at the time stamp to determine which of the backups is the most recent.

After restoring the backup, sync the iPhone XR to your computer, and then eject the drive.

iCloud Backup

Power on your iPhone XR and choose your country and language. You will be asked to choose how you want to set up the device, either from an Android device, as a new iPhone or to restore settings and data from a backup.

Choose iCloud backup.

Enter the login details for your Apple ID account.

If you have turned on two-factor authentication, you should get an alert on any of your devices that are running iOS 10 or advanced models, or your MacBook, if it is running macOS Sierra or advanced models like macOS High Sierra and macOS Mojave.

Enter the code provided on your iPhone.

Read and agree to the terms and conditions.

Look through the iCloud backups that you have, and going by the time stamp, choose the most recent.

Once you have selected the desired backup, decide whether you want to customize your settings on your new iPhone XR, or if you want to replicate the same settings you had on the old iPhone.

Your iPhone XR will then restore settings from the chosen iCloud backup.

Remember that this process might take a while, depending on how strong your internet connection is. You can step away for a cup of coffee while you wait.

Chapter 7: iPhone XR Tips and Tricks

The iPhone XR is a unique device in the line of iPhone products. Retailing below $1,000, it is the first device that has Face ID and an edge-to-edge design. This is a device that is simply designed for use by everyone. Whether you are upgrading from an iPhone 6 or an iPhone 8, this is the device you should run to.

There is a lot that you can learn to help you get the utmost utility from this device. It might take you a while to get used to the tweaks, but once you do, this will be one of the best mobile experiences you have had in years. The following are some useful tips that will help you make the most use of your phone.

Waking your phone up

Unlike the previous devices, iPhone XR has a Tap to Wake feature. If you do not want to fiddle with the side button, tap on the screen and it will wake up. This is ideal if you want to check notifications and get back to whatever you were doing.

Accessing Home

The Home button is conspicuously missing in the iPhone XR. To access Home, swipe up on your screen from the bottom. This gesture will also unlock your iPhone XR.

App Switcher

To access App Switcher, swipe up from your Home bar, but hold on briefly. However, for an on-the-go user, this is a waste of time. Instead of doing this, swipe up on your screen from the left edge at 45 degrees. This gets you to the App Switcher.

Accessing the Notification Center

To view your notifications from the notification center, swipe down from the notch area.

Accessing Control Center

Swipe down from either the right ear or right edge close to the notch to access the Control Center. From here, you can customize settings as you please to include settings for Accessibility, your Apple TV remote and so forth.

Making Payments

Using Apple Pay for payments is very easy. Press your side button twice – it is on the right side of the phone. Hold your iPhone XR to your face and use Face ID to scan your face.

Switching between Recent Apps

The iPhone XR comes with a Quick App switcher gesture. With this, you can switch between your recent apps seamlessly. To access an app you used previously, swipe right. Keep swiping to access the apps further. A left swipe takes you back to the app you accessed first.

This only works if you do not interact with any app. If you do, the system detects, and you have to swipe right to access the one you were using previously. This is a simple process, but it can be confusing. You will need some practice to familiarize yourself with it.

Taking Screenshots

You do not have a Home button on the iPhone XR, so taking a

screenshot the traditional way is not possible. For screenshots, press and hold the volume down button and the side button.

Using Siri

The easiest way to access Siri is to press and hold the Side button. Alternatively, if you are not comfortable with this setting, you can set up Hey Siri for additional functionality.

Rebooting your device

The lack of a home button makes some mundane tasks on the iPhone seem complicated, like rebooting your phone. Hold the side button and any of the volume buttons to reboot your device.

Perform a hard reset

There is nothing special about a hard reset. It is but an elevated reboot. In case you were wondering, a hard reset does not erase data from your phone. Press volume up, volume down, then press and hold the side button until the Apple logo appears on your screen.

Creating Memojis

Emojis have been delightful highlights to many conversations. With the Face ID and the TrueDepth camera on the iPhone XR, you get to animate your emojis and make conversations more entertaining. The Memoji is an advanced form of emoji that is more fun to work with. When using a Memoji, you are creating a Bitmoji-like character on your phone. To create a Memoji, go to Messages, choose any iMessage chat and click on the Animoji app, then proceed.

Depth Effect Selfies

Having an iPhone with an amazing camera sensor is a good thing.

You are able to take amazing selfies with depth effect. On your camera, change to portrait mode and flip your iPhone XR for this unique selfie.

Managing notifications from your lock screen

The iOS 12 brings advanced user abilities to the iPhone XR. From your lock screen, you can access and manage notifications. To do this, swipe left on any notification notice and tap Manage.

This is where you can turn off notifications for apps that you do not need to receive frequently. Other settings include Deliver Quietly, where the app does not show notifications on your lock screen. Your phone will not make a sound if the app has any notifications. However, to access such notifications, you must open the Notification Center.

Two, - Pane Landscape View

The two-pane landscape view is characteristic of the iPhone XS Max. Apple also introduced this in the iPhone XR. On your phone, perhaps you are accessing Mail, and you also need to keep track of some notes, just flip your phone to the side, and you will get the same two-pane view that you should be familiar with when using an iPad.

Face ID Fails

As amazing as Face ID is, at times it becomes a bother when it gets wonky. If you try to initiate Face ID and it fails, you can give it a second try. Do not enter your passcode just yet, instead, swipe up and you will get the settings right.

Multiple Face ID Faces

iOS 12 allows you to register more than one face for Face ID. Perhaps you need to share your phone with your partner, so this would come in handy. All you need to do is add a second face to your Face ID settings.

Go to Settings, select Face ID, then Set Up an Alternative Appearance. Your iPhone XR will give you prompts to follow, until you are done setting up a second face.

Bring back the Home Button

While some people have made peace with the fact that the Home Button is no more, others cannot move on that easily. If swipe gestures to enjoy Home Button services are not your thing, you can use the AssistiveTouch Home Button. This is a virtual feature that allows you to bring back the home button.

Go to Settings, then Accessibility, and select AssistiveTouch. From here, you can create shortcuts for 3D Touch, long press, single tap, and double tap. You can define unique gestures for different responses.

Editing Depth from Portrait Shots

Your iPhone XR might only come with one camera, but this does not limit you from getting the most out of it. Having taken photos, you can still edit them later on with depth effect. In photo view, tap on edit and use the slider at the bottom of the screen to alter the depth effect as you desire.

Setting up Fast Charge

The iPhone XR comes with a 5W charger. For someone who uses their phone all the time, it will run out of juice. The iPhone XR supports a fast charge, so a fast charger will come in handy. If you have an iPad, you can use your 12W charger for your iPhone XR.

Taking RAW photos

The default iPhone camera is decent as it is. You can do so much with it, without any added settings. However, if you need full control of things like shutter speed, focus, and exposure, you must install a third-party application. One of the best for this is Halide, which allows you to take RAW photos.

Shortcuts for task automation

The iPhone XR is one of the smartest devices you will ever get in the market at the moment. Some tasks, especially repetitive ones, can be automated. You can also group others together. The Shortcuts app helps you create shortcuts that can, among other things, send messages, read headlines, change the Do Not Disturb mode, turn off the lights and so forth, all with a single command.

Water Resistance

In a market that has a lot of phones that are capable of doing amazing things underwater, the iPhone XR is not one of them. This is an IP67 phone, which means that it is only splash resistant. Do not take it swimming. If it happens to drop in water, do not let it stay submerged for a long time. At the same time, resist the temptation to use your phone underwater.

Protection from theft and loss

You can lose your phone in different circumstances. With Apple Care+ Theft and Loss Protection, you do not need to worry about these anymore. It will cost you $249, but if you ever lose your iPhone XR, or if it is stolen, you can get a replacement. The good thing about this plan is that you can break it down in manageable installments.

Message Previews on your Lock Screen

How do you want to access your messages? Previews are a good thing. They help you brush through messages without having to lose time reading all of them. By default, your iPhone XR does not show message previews until you scan your face with Face ID. In terms of privacy, this is an awesome feature.

However, some people who need instant access to message previews feel this is too much. For those who prefer the screen waking up irrespective of the angle to access the notifications, using Face ID to preview messages can be a bother. You can disable this easily. Navigate to Settings, then Notifications, and select Show Previews, then choose Always.

Chapter 8: iPhone XR vs iPhone XS

A lot has been said about the iPhone XR, especially when pitting it against iPhone XS. There are shared features and some dissimilarities here and there. Overall, however, these are two amazing phones. The release of the iPhone XR was marked by a lot of expectation, being that it was an exciting device, and at an affordable price.

Choosing between an iPhone and an Android device is often an easy choice because you are probably looking at the price, the brand you are loyal to, unique features, and so forth. However, if you have to choose between two or more iPhone devices, it can be quite a challenge. Price alone cannot be the deciding factor. You have to go deeper, learn more about the devices so that you make an informed decision. This comparison will pit the iPhone XR and iPhone XS.

Display

One of the first things you notice when comparing an iPhone XR and an iPhone XS is the display disparities. The iPhone XS has a smaller screen than the iPhone XR. Which one is better of the two?

Someone who fancies large screen devices will go for the iPhone XR. However, what are you getting in an iPhone XR that you cannot find in an iPhone XS, in light of the screen? Is a big screen always the better option in terms of experience and utility?

Experts contend that the iPhone XR screen is inferior to the iPhone XS. The iPhone XS has an OLED screen at 5.8 inches. The iPhone XR only has an LCD screen, at 6.1 inches.

Other than the dimensions according to size, you get True Tone 2436 x 1125 pixels at 458 ppi on the iPhone XS, compared to the True Tone 1792 x 828 pixels at 326 ppi on the iPhone XR.

The contrast ratio on the iPhone XS is 1,000,000:1 versus 1,400:1 on the iPhone XR. The screen to body ratio is 82.9% on the iPhone XS, compared to 79.0% on the iPhone XR.

Based on the display parameters, the iPhone XR is a downgrade from OLED to LCD, compromising on a few displays comforts that most iPhone users are used to. The resolution on the iPhone XR is significantly lower. It gets so bad, and you cannot experience full HD content at 1080p on the iPhone XR. For a device that boasts of 6.1 inches of screen surface, this is a let-down. There are many devices in the market that offer far superior display parameters for a fraction of what Apple is charging for the iPhone XR.

Since the introduction of iPhone 6S, 3D Touch technology has been a prominent feature in iPhones, which is surprisingly missing in the iPhone XR. However, Apple makes up for this by making it HDR10 and Dolby Vision compliant just like the iPhone XS. This is brilliant, especially since you are able to enjoy high-quality videos on the iPhone XR.

Looking at the OLED screens, an LCD screen might not be able to pack a punch, especially when you are looking at the black levels and contrast ratio. However, for many an average iPhone user, the LCD screen is more than sufficient.

Just in case you feel the 326 ppi is not sufficient, a kind reminder would suffice, that it was the same resolution depth that was used in the iconic iPhone 8. Besides, 326 ppi is more than what you would get in a 40" 4K TV, which only serves you 110 ppi. The aspect ratio on the iPhone XR is still the same as what you get on the iPhone XS, 19:5:9. The iPhone XR also gets a True Tone color accuracy, with 120 Hz touch sensing, which allows you to enjoy a more responsive touch input.

iOS 12 brings forth a lot of advancements that make it easier for you to enjoy a variety of functions that would have been missing without 3D Touch. On the brighter side, however, there has been a slow uptake and appreciation of 3D Touch from users, and in response, Apple is shelving it altogether. In retrospect, the display is one of the biggest differences between the iPhone XR and the iPhone XS, though most people will barely care about it.

Model design and finishes

When you look at the iPhone XR and iPhone XS, the two devices almost look similar. However, they are not. There is a very small difference between the two devices:

iPhone XR - 150.9 x 75.7 x 8.3 mm (5.94 x 2.98 x 0.33 in) and 194 g (6.84 oz)

iPhone XS - 143.6 x 70.9 x 7.7 mm (5.65 x 2.79 x 0.30 in) and 177g (6.24 oz)

As you can see, the iPhone XR is slightly larger than the iPhone XR, but this also means an additional 10% in weight. This is attributed to the weight of the LCD display screen. The LCD is traditionally less flexible compared to OLED displays, which means you cannot fit it comfortably into the iPhone chassis. This explains the presence of larger bezels on the sides of the iPhone XR.

The iPhone XS gets a premium feel thanks to the stainless steel chassis, making it a fancier option than the iPhone XR. The iPhone XR features a 7000 series aluminum chassis, the same model that was used in the iPhone 8 and the predecessor models. The iPhone XR only gets an IP67 water resistance rating, compared to the IP68 water resistance rating that is used in the iPhone XS.

The IP68 rating allows you to submerge the iPhone XS in water for no more than half an hour if the water depth is no more than two meters. These are simple features that most average users would not give a care about. On the bright side, while the iPhone XR has thicker bezels compared to the iPhone XS, they still come out thinner than most of the other OLED devices that are available in the market.

Both of the devices have external stereo speakers on the left and right, which deliver 25% louder sound than their predecessors. They also have dual SIM support, and you can use an internal eSIM or a nano SIM. Therefore, you can use both your home and travel sim on the same device. The good thing about this is that it is a feature that has never been present in any iPhone device since the beginning of time.

In terms of the appeal, iPhone XS comes limited to three colors, (Gold, Space Grey, and Silver) while iPhone XR is available in six colors (Coral, Yellow, Blue, Black, White, and Red). If you are the kind of user who appreciates diversity and something that gives you true perspective, the iPhone XR is your best bet. It has even been dubbed a more interesting model of the iPhones released in 2018.

Performance

One of the things that you will appreciate about the iPhone XR is the fact that it is running the same chipset that powers the iPhone XS. These two devices are all running Apple's A12 bionic chipset.

The chipset features a six-core CPU, four core GPU, and an M12 motion coprocessor.

What sets them differently that the iPhone XS is loaded with 4 GB of memory, but the iPhone XR comes in a distant second with only 3 GB. Where will you feel this difference? Most people will barely notice. However, if you are someone who likes to multitask on their device, over time, you will notice a slight lag in performance.

It might not be apparent, especially when you are running light apps. However, if you are a gamer, or you use a lot of apps that are resource intensive, you will notice a difference. The reason why your apps will lag in performance is that you have a lot of them hogging your memory space, without allowing the device to reload.

The experts at Apple do contend, however, that there is a good reason why the iPhone XS was fitted with a larger RAM than the iPhone XR. The iPhone XS has two cameras. It needs additional memory resources to power the dual camera functions. If you want to know that 3 GB on the iPhone XR is not something to frown upon, take a step back and think about the iPhone X. This device was loaded with 3 GB of RAM, but you will not come across people complaining that it is a slow device.

Demystifying the A12 Bionic Chipset

What is so special about this chipset? The term bionic attached to the name is a pure marketing gimmick. However, that should not take away the important points about this chipset. Ideally, what you are getting through this chipset is a 50% improvement in power efficiency when your iPhone XR is running idle, or in terms of the graphics performance. Other than that, you will get an improvement in the CPU performance, of up to 15% based on the predecessor model.

There is a good reason why the A12 chipset is setting Apple, and all devices that are running it, a cut above the rest. In terms of competition, iPhone X, released in 2017 is considerably faster than any other Android device that was released in 2018. This means that Apple is just that good. They do not need the power, but they are giving it to you because they can.

Whether you are getting the iPhone XR or the iPhone XS, you will appreciate the power reserve capacity in the device. How important is this to you? Power reserves help you with NFC transactions. You should be able to complete the transactions even when your battery has run out. This is a feature that Apple has built into all the devices that were released in 2018, and hopefully will be a mainstay in the future, with a few improvements, of course.

Back in the day, iPhones were built incompatible with 600 MHz 4G bands. These bands are useful especially in areas where there was no signal. Apple has built this into the iPhone XR and the iPhone XS. This is a step in the right direction, opening up new frontiers for the tech giant.

However, even though the iPhone XR is able to support 4G, it is not fitted with the 4G Cat 16 LTE speed that is built into the iPhone XS. With this support, the iPhone XS can support downloads up to one gigabit. To be honest, this is too much power in one device. However, even without that, the iPhone XR still has a Cat 12 600 Mbit speed support, whose power is more than most average users need on their devices. There are credible reports that Apple might still be lagging behind in terms of adding 5G support to their devices. However, if you are getting such amazing speeds on your 4G enabled device, there is no reason for you to worry.

Cameras

Everything about the iPhone XR and the iPhone XS is the same when we consider optics, especially the dual rear camera. Other than the differences in display size, the only other feature that you can recognize almost immediately between these two is that the iPhone XR only has one rear camera. Let's take a closer look at the camera specifications of these two devices:

They both have a primary rear camera, 12MP, f/1.8 aperture, 1.4μm pixel size. The camera supports Optical Image stabilization (OIS), Quad-LED True Tone flash, and Portrait Lighting.

While the iPhone XR does not have a secondary rear camera, the iPhone XS has a secondary telephoto lens with the following features: 12MP, f/2.4 aperture, 1.0μm pixel size, OIS, and 2x optical zoom.

For the front camera, the two devices both have a TrueDepth camera, 7MP, f/2.2 aperture

Is it a good thing that the iPhone XR does not have 2x optical zoom on it? Some people would agree, others would be indecisive. However, how often do you need to zoom into an object to capture it? Most people just move closer to the object and take awesome shots. Bearing this in mind, you might not really miss it.

If we look at some of the earlier models, they all needed a secondary camera to help in taking good Portrait Mode shots. The iPhone XR, however, is capable of doing this with the rear and single front cameras, so you will do just fine with it.

One other thing that Apple has done on the iPhone XR and the iPhone XS is to offer HDR image processing. The beauty of HDR image processing is that you are able to combine lots of photos taken from unique exposure angles and combine them into one image. This feature was built into the devices to address an issue that Apple devices have always had since time immemorial, a weakness with dynamic range. With this in mind, the iPhone XR and iPhone XS can offer the same experience you would enjoy when you are using a Google Pixel 2, which has been dubbed one of the phones with the best cameras.

Both of the iPhones have an enlarged pixel size on the primary rear cameras. A larger pixel size makes them allow more light in, which is an important upgrade to improve photography in low light settings.

Charging and battery life

A lot of people often expect that they will get longer battery life on a more expensive device. This is not the case when you compare the iPhone XR and the iPhone XS. In terms of the battery life, we have to go back to the OLED and LCD comparison and learn something important. An LCD display does not consume as many resources as an OLED display.

The upside to using an LCD display on the iPhone XR over the OLED display used in the iPhone XS is that you are getting a low resolution on the XR than the XS. A low resolution consumes less power, and since the phone comes in a large size, Apple has enough room to load the device with a larger battery.

On the iPhone XR, you are getting 2,942 mAh, while the iPhone XS only offers 2,658 mAh. Why is this important? The iPhone XR, running this battery, is capable of lasting 25% longer than the iPhone XS on most functions. In fact, the iPhone XR can even outlast the iPhone XS Max, yet this was the flagship model.

However, there is a catch when it comes to the iPhone XR. It does not support fast wireless charging. Whether or not users will struggle to accept this, we will probably see in the next rollout of iPhone devices.

For wired charging, both the iPhone XR and iPhone XS are supported. If your device is flat out, you can get it up to 50% charging in half an hour. However, in traditional fashion, Apple still refuses to include a fast charger in the box when you buy the phone. You have to fork out an additional $75 to get the compatible cable and fast charger.

Cost consideration

If you need a wired fast charger for your devices, you will need to consider adding another $75 to your purchase price. However, that aside, the iPhone XR is still popular as the most affordable Apple device in its range.

This is how the devices compare:

iPhone XS

- 64GB at $999

- 256GB at $1,149

- 512GB at $1,349

iPhone XR

- 64GB at $749

- 128GB at $799

- 256GB at $899

Chapter 9: iPhone XR Out of the Box

Apple has bundled quite a few things inside the box. Here's a list of things you can expect to take out of the box.

IPhone XR

This is what you paid your money for. So make sure that you do not lose it.

Lightning to USB Cable

Apple is still using the charging connector it introduced with the iPhone 5 which launched in 2012. Although other members of the family have switched to the conveniently smaller USB-C connector, the iPhone XR still comes with the regular USB connector.

Five-Watt Charging Adapter

The box comes with a five-watt charging adapter. While there are other charging blocks available in the market that offer a faster charge, the one that is in the box will offer the same charging speed as the previous ones released by Apple.

Ear Pods With A Lightning Connector

The 3.5mm headphone jack has been history ever since Apple introduced the iPhone 7 in 2016 and the case is the same as the new iPhone XR. The ear pods provided with the iPhone XR team up with the lightning connector to plug into the charging port offering access to music and other audio features. Since the connectors are not compatible with the universal 3.5mm connector, you are restricted to use the earpods with the iPhone.

Kindly note that the Ear Pods are not AirPods that cost $159 and are wireless in nature. We did expect Apple to introduce a newer version of the Ear Pods in their September 2018 conference, but there was no sign of any such launch at the event.

Another point to be noted is that Apple has not offered the dongle for the 3.5mm adapter to lightning cable in the box and you will need to get your own from Apple at $9 or from any 3rd party vendor. So if you don't have Bluetooth Earphones, or if you do not want to use the set that came bundled along in the box, you will have to shell out the extra dollars to reconnect your non-Apple headphones or earphones.

Overall Performance Notes

If your decision to purchase an iPhone was only based on benchmark scores, it is totally fine if you wonder why anyone would want to go for an iPhone XS and not purchase the iPhone XR. The performance is the same, the battery life is shorter and the damage to the pocket is $250 more.

However, the quality of an iPhone is determined by factors more than just benchmark scores. The iPhone XS has

1. High-resolution OLED display with HDR support

2. Dual rear cameras for portrait pictures

3. 3D touch

4. Better Waterproofing

5. More storage options

6. 4GB of RAM as compared to the 3GB on iPhone XR

The difference in RAM did not show much of an impact in the benchmark results but it will be something that will affect performance over the years.

The best thing about the iPhone XR is that its benchmarks, unlike iPhone 5C, which was the cheap model of that particular year, do not compromise on performance or battery despite being the cheapest model of 2018. Therefore, we can keep reiterating that the iPhone XR has had the best battery life an iPhone ever had. Therefore, there are very low chances of the iPhone XR becoming obsolete before the iPhone XS does.

Chapter 10: Initial Setup

Regardless of whether you are upgrading your iPhone for the latest iPhone XR or are a first-time Apple user, it is time to set up your new iPhone. The process of setting up the iPhone can be rather exhilarating, pretty much like waking up on Christmas morning and unwrapping all the presents placed under the Christmas tree. There are numerous features that you can explore, but before you can do this, you need to set up your iPhone. From the instant you see the first "Hello" displayed on your screen until the final step, here is everything that you must know about setting up your brand-new iPhone XR.

Different Options

When you are setting up your new iPhone, there are three options that you can use, and they are - starting over again, restoring the data from another iPhone, or even by importing the data from a non-iOS phone. If you wish to start anew, it means that you will need to set up your phone as a completely new device and must start changing all the settings. You must opt for this option if you have never used a smartphone before or you want to make it feel like your iPhone is brand-new, in a literal sense. You can restore the data that you have backed up on the iCloud or iTunes from any previous iOS backed device like an iPhone, iPad or even an iPod touch. You must opt for this if you are an existing iOS device user and are upgrading to the latest model of the iPhone. If you are a current user of a smartphone that's powered by Android, BlackBerry or Windows, then you might need to transfer all the data from your previous phone to your new iPhone XR.

Chapter 11: Start the Set-Up

As soon as you power up your iPhone for the first time, you will be greeted by a pleasant "Hello" on your screen in different languages. This one thing stays the same regardless of whether you are setting up your iPhone as a new device, are importing data from a non-iOS device, or are transferring the data from another iPhone.

- The first thing that you must do is place your finger on the "slide to set up" option on your screen and gently slide your finger across the iPhone's screen to start.

- Now, you need to select your language. Select a language of your choice from the extensive list that's displayed on your screen.

- Once you do this, you must select your region or country.

- The fourth step is to configure your network settings. You must opt for "Wi-Fi" network unless you are not within the range of a Wi-fFi network, then you can opt for the "Cellular" instead of "Wi-Fi network."

As soon as you do this, you have the option of setting up your iPhone XR using the passcode and settings you used on your previous iPhone. To do this, you must select the "Automatic Setup" option. If you want to set up your new iPhone XR as a brand-new device, then here are the steps that you can follow.

- Once you read the Data and Privacy policies of Apple, please select "continue."

- Click on "Enable Location Services." If you aren't interested in enabling the location services at the moment, you can click on the "Skip Location Services" option for now. You can enable these services later.

- Now, it is time to create the Face ID for your iPhone XR. This is quite easy; you merely need to make sure that you can view your face in the circle that's displayed on the screen. Move your head around gradually to complete the circle. Once this is done, the device will inform you about it.

- You need to set a Passcode for your new device. You can either use a regular 6-digit passcode, a 4-digit passcode, or even customize your passcode by selecting the "Passcode Options."

If you wish to start afresh, it means that you will need to set up your phone as a completely new device and must start changing all the settings. You must choose this option if you have never used a smartphone before or you want to make it feel like your iPhone is brand-new, in a literal sense. Here are the steps:

Set Up as a New iPhone → Apple ID and Password (You can easily create one by following the instructions displayed on your screen).

Read and then tap "Agree" to Apple's T&Cs.

Now, set up Apple Pay, iCloud Keychain, and Siri.

You can restore the data that you have backed up on the iCloud or iTunes from any previous iOS backed device like an iPhone, iPad or even iPod touch. You must opt for this if you are an existing iOS device user and are upgrading to the latest model of the iPhone. If you wish to restore your apps and data from another iPhone, then you have two options available - either use iCloud or iTunes. This choice depends on whether you used to backup your previous iPhone in iCloud or by plugging it to your computer and then backing it up using iTunes. Before you can choose either of these, ensure that your previous iPhone is backed up. Now, you merely need to determine whether you wish to restore data and apps using iCloud or iTunes.

If you are an existing user of a smartphone that's powered by Android, BlackBerry or Windows, then you might need to transfer all the data from your previous phone to your new iPhone XR. To do this, you must use an app provided by Apple known as "Move to iOS," and it is now available in the Google Play store. Before you can transfer the data to your iPhone, please download this app on your existing Android phone and follow the steps as the app guides you.

Chapter 12: iPhone XR Battery

This is probably the test you've wanted to see results for all along because this is where the iPhone XR produces interesting results. If you compared the iPhone XS to the iPhone Max, the battery consumption considered was fairly simple. The iPhone XS Max is the same phone like the iPhone XS which is just bigger in size and therefore comes with a battery which is 3174 mAh as compared to the 2658 mAh on the iPhone XS. The pixel density and the OLED technology stands the same on both the phones. The end result shows that the iPhone XS Max gets an additional hour of screen time in comparison with the iPhone XS.

As opposed to iPhone XS and XS Max, the iPhone XR is a completely different matter when it comes to battery life. The 6.1-inch display is the intermediate between the 5.8-inch screen of the XS and 6.5-inch screen of the XS Max. The battery with 2942 mAh also falls between the battery capacities of its siblings. But the difference is in the display as the iPhone XR comes with an LCD instead of an OLED like its siblings and has a pixel density of 326 pixels per inch which is less in comparison to its siblings which have a pixel density of 458 pixels per inch. The power utilization from the processor is the same as the other models but the iPhone XR saves battery on its display.

Something you will fancy about the iPhone XR is drawing comparisons with the XS and XS Max, especially since you are paying much less to get it.

Let's have a look at the battery. The XR features a 2,942 mAh battery. Of course, this comes nowhere close to the flagship iPhones with a battery capacity of more than 4,000 mAh. However, why is this important? Well, the XS only runs a 2,658 mAh battery. So, for a few bucks less, you are getting more juice out of the XR. The XS Max, however, features a 3,174 mAh battery.

The official battery specifications for the iPhone XR according to Apple are as follows:

- Up to 25 hours talk time on wireless

- Up to 15 hours on Internet use

- Up to 16 hours video playback on wireless

- Up to 65 hours audio playback on wireless

Compared to the iPhone 8 Plus, you have around one and a half hours more battery life, which makes it a good idea for someone who is looking for an upgrade.

Also, a bonus, Apple also included wireless charging on the iPhone XR.

Battery Life

iPhone XR: 333

iPhone XS: 264

iPhone XS Max: 314

iPhone X: 257

IDG

The iPhone XR has a battery that has proved to be the best among all the iPhones that exist in the market currently.

The test is not an ideal everyday scenario but an intensive power draining case where the screen is always on and the CPU and GPU are kept under continuous load. In an ideal scenario where you use it on a daily basis, you will end up getting much longer battery life than the results you see in this test, especially if the tasks and apps being used on the phone are simple. So this test does not serve as a perfect analogy to everyday use of the iPhone XR but helps you understand the difference in battery life as compared to the siblings of the iPhone X family.

The test between the iPhones of the X-family yielded the following results.

1. The iPhone XR lasted 19 minutes longer in comparison to the iPhone XS Max.

2. The iPhone XR lasted 60+ minutes longer than the iPhone XS.

In a real-world routine, where you are not purposely draining the battery life, the above result will translate to about 30-45 minutes of more screen time in comparison with the iPhone XS Max and around 2 hours more as compared to that of the iPhone XS, depending upon the usage pattern on your phone.

Thus, we can safely say that the iPhone XR holds a better charge than any other iPhone available in the market today.

An interesting test with the iPhone 7 showed the following results for the iPhone XR when we compared battery life.

1. The iPhone XR and the iPhone 7 have almost the same battery size, which is around 2900mAh.

2. Both of the phones have an LCD display with almost the same area. The display on the iPhone XR is 90 square centimeters while that on iPhone 7 is 83 square centimeters, which is only 7 percent smaller.

Even after such marginal differences, the iPhone XR lasted an hour and 45 minutes longer in the above-mentioned test.

This implies at least a 45 percent improvement in battery life from the iPhone 7 to the iPhone XR even after providing a larger display. This is a big achievement by Apple in a period of 2 years.

Chapter 13: iPhone XR Display

The iPhone XR display is one of the features that has got many people talking. Many people have by now experienced the OLED screens that are popular in the market and would have expected the iPhone XR to follow suit. However, Apple decided to go with an LCD screen.

The iPhone XR, instead of going the OLED way as it has been witnessed in models like the iPhone X and iPhone XS, was built with LCD screens. It is an interesting decision, given that LCD screens are considered a thing of the past. However, according to Apple, the LCD used in the iPhone XR is more of a futuristic approach.

Why would Apple go this way? It is important to note that Apple still stays true to the LCD screens as their standard display technology for their devices. Even with an LCD screen in the face of OLED competition, Apple still takes a win with the XR, given that they have designed a device that, for the very first time, has the entire front face of the camera covered. On the iPhone XR, it has been tagged the Liquid Retina display. What this means is that Apple has done away with the chin and forehead design that users have been accustomed to for a long time.

Perhaps the screen is not one of the most amazing features of the iPhone XR. While the other phones in its class come with amazing OLED displays, it only comes with an LCD screen. The 6.1 inches in your hands will perhaps make up for this if you fancy a gigantic screen. The thing with LCD screens is that they are not as bright as OLED screens. So, other than the massive screen in your hand, you should not expect the crisp, liquid clear clarity you will find in the XS and XS Max.

What makes this LCD screen different from archaic models? The screen on the iPhone XR, like the OLED screens, is rounded from one corner to the other. It features subpixel and masking skills, and an additional LED back-lighting. The backlight on the iPhone XR LCD screen helps to support lightning depression and also helps to make up for the lack of 3D Touch for Haptic Touch.

Concerning screen size, the iPhone XR is, in fact, the second largest device that Apple has released. It is sandwiched in size by the iPhone XS Max and the iPhone XS. The iPhone XR comes with 6.1 inches of screen size, which is a big deal compared to 5.8 inches that we have seen in the iPhone X and iPhone XS.

If you have been looking for an upgrade in screen size, the iPhone XR will make a good candidate. It is only second to the iPhone XS Max, which comes in at 6.5 inches. For many iPhone users, 6.1 inches is an ideal size, given that people have been asking for a long time whether Apple would follow in the footsteps of the Android competitors and release widescreen phones.

The iPhone market is advancing in light of consumer demands, and a big screen is considered something most people are looking for. There are a number of users who still appreciate the smaller devices, like the iPhone SE. However, the fact remains that people are looking forward to bigger devices, and for a good reason.

In recent years, we have seen larger phones eat into the market share for tablets, killing smaller size tablets in the process. A big screen is, considered an appropriate device that cuts across cultural and gender divides, hence the 6.1 inches on the iPhone XR is a welcome move.

We must also appreciate the fact that phones are currently one of the key communications and computing devices for most people, and the move toward a bigger screen is about increasing creativity and productivity.

Building on the screen size, the iPhone XR shares a lot of advantages with the iPhone XS Max. One of these features is Display Zoom, a feature that is designed to make the device more accessible. With Display Zoom, it is easier to see things clearly on the large screen. Interactions are enhanced, and your touch capacity is also improved. This is also designed to help you navigate faster when using the iPhone XR, especially when you are going through lists with finer details.

A large screen is only as good as you can enjoy utility value from it. With the iPhone XR, you can enjoy reachability, accessing the top of your phone screen from the middle. The iPhone XR employs the X-style navigation system for gestures. It might take a while getting used to this, but when you do, you will be able to enjoy the Home button experience.

For all the good things that have been said about the iPhone XR, there is not much to look forward to about the resolution and density, unless this is your first experience with an iPhone. Those who have used iPhones over the years will notice the differences.

The iPhone XS and iPhone XS Max both feature impressive screen resolutions, at 2436 x 1125 and 2688 x 1942 respectively, with 458 ppi. The iPhone XR, on the other hand, features a paltry 1792 x 828 resolution, with 326 ppi.

It might not feel right comparing an OLED screen with an LCD screen, especially when you look at the foundational design and build of the screens. They are two different technologies. When addressing the differences in terms of the advantages and disadvantages of LCD and OLED screens, the disparities are at best, relative. It would take a lot to put them side by side in a fair comparison.

A lot of people would feel an LCD screen is a step back, but this is not true. There are challenges that are faced by the OLED screens too. Some of the common challenges that you would experience when using an OLED screen include an off-axis color shift and black smearing. With an LCD screen, you do not have to worry about black smearing or off-axis color shift. That being said, however, LCD is simply not as alluring and desirable as an OLED screen. OLED screens offer an amazing deep black hue and a high contrast range that you would never experience in the LCD screen on the iPhone XR.

What Apple has done with the iPhone XR is to give the LCD a new lease of life, pushing it as far as they can. You can, however, not expect to get the HDR (high dynamic range) experience, but the color scheme and calibration in the iPhone XR is amazing. On this feature, the iPhone XR offers pretty much the same experience you would get in an iPhone XS.

The display on the iPhone XR is not 1080p. This does not mean you will not get an amazing experience with this device. However, unless you plan on using VR on your device where you should be getting 4K on either eye, the 326 ppi available with the iPhone XR is decent, especially for normal viewing distances.

For normal use, however, you should not notice any difference when using the iPhone XR. It is a fantastic device which promises to deliver an amazing user experience.

Chapter 14: Camera and Resolution

The camera is one of the key features a lot of people consider if they plan to buy an iPhone, and the iPhone XR is no different. The camera built into the iPhone XR is leveraged on the power of the A12 chip, delivering some fantastic capabilities.

You are getting a 7-megapixel selfie camera, which is the same specification used in the iPhone XS and iPhone XS Max. What you might not be able to enjoy, however, is the zoom feature. The picture quality is not as good as you would expect in an iPhone.

You have a 12-megapixel rear camera on the iPhone XR. All you can do with this camera is a digital zoom. The problem with cameras that are limited to digital zoom is that the quality can be grainy. This is a concern, especially when you compare the iPhone XR with iPhone XS and iPhone XS Max, which have a telephoto lens with optical zoom. The camera on the iPhone XR, however, gets saved by the A12 bionic chip. This powerful processor allows you to edit the depth of field in your photos after your shots.

The power behind the A12 bionic processor is responsible for the amazing graphics performance, real-time machine learning, and amazing photo processing capabilities that you get with the iPhone XR. This device also features an improved image signal processor and improved sensors. While it only has a 12 MP camera that has been a mainstay for many years, you can still enjoy detailed photos. With the Smart HDR function, you can improve your photos thanks to machine learning. Even though you only have one camera on the iPhone XR, you can still take decent photos in portrait mode.

The iPhone XR has a resolution of 1792 x 828 pixels, with a 326 ppi density. The iPhone XS, on the other hand, has a 2436 x 1125 resolution, and a 458 ppi. What this means is that with the iPhone XR, you can only enjoy watching videos up to 828p. This is good for most of the videos you can come across during your mobile experience. However, if you are looking to enjoy an unrivaled YouTube or Netflix experience on your iPhone XR, you might be slightly disappointed. You should, however, still be able to render most games on the iPhone without a hitch.

Here is a detailed report of how the single lens camera on the iPhone XR compares to all the other phone cameras in the world right now. We will deep dive into the iPhone XR camera and perform tests on the various features of the camera to see how good it is.

The iPhone XR offers a single-lens camera for photography, as opposed to the dual-lens setup that can be found on the iPhone XS models. If we look at the specifications of the camera on the iPhone XR, it gives us exactly what one can expect from a top of the line, single lens device featuring the following.

- 12MP

- A 1/2.55″ sensor which has a 1.4μm pixel pitch

- 26mm f/1.8 aperture lens which comes along with optical image stabilization

- Dual Tone LED Flash

- Phase-detection autofocus (PDAF)

- 4K videos at 24/30/60 fps (1080p at 30 fps at default

settings)

Although there is a difference in hardware of the camera, when we look at the image processing and the software side of things, the iPhone XR is equipped with the same technology as the iPhone XS models.

A professional camera, when capturing stills, tends to capture a multi-frame buffer using different exposures, which facilitates zero lag on the shutter and HDR processing. This technology is available on the latest iPhones including the iPhone XR and therefore it has the ability to display HDR image on your screen in real time. This simply means that you end up getting a preview image true to the saying "what you see is what you get."

DxOMark Tests

DxOMark is a website providing image quality ratings for standalone cameras, lenses, and mobile devices that include cameras, particularly smartphones. Let's go through the rating DxOMark provided for the single-lens camera on the iPhone XR.

Exposure and Contrast: 90

The iPhone XR gets a good exposure score since it provides a wide dynamic range through both indoor and outdoor conditions along with accurate exposures. If the lighting is very bright with an increase in contrast scenes, the HDR triggers automatically in the default mode of the camera resulting in capturing detailed pictures in both the darkest and brightest regions. The HDR results on the iPhone XR are at par with that of the iPhone XS Max, having a slight difference, but still, the iPhone XR retains more highlight fractionally as compared to the Pixel 2 by Google.

The iPhone XR provides excellent target exposures even at very low light at 20 lux. The target exposure is a little less than ideal when the light conditions drop down to very low such as 1 to 5 lux, but you will still get images that are very usable. The iPhone XS Max provides marginally better target exposure even at 1 lux, which is why it gets an upper hand over its sibling in the exposure department.

The iPhone XR is very good with exposure of faces even when there is a lot of background light, proving that the image processing algorithms work as intended. Target exposure is almost accurate indoors where the lighting is accompanied with good contrast and details are preserved well through the highlight in the regions with shadow.

Color: 82

The iPhone XR ends up rendering vibrant and saturated colors, especially in outdoor lighting conditions, resulting in the hues really popping up. In low light conditions, colors remain subtle but are still pleasant to the eyes.

The color saturation remains very good in low light shots at around 20 lux and is just a tad bit behind the Pixel 2 and the iPhone XS Max. The Pixel 2 has a white balance that looks greener under fluorescent lighting which makes its white look cleaner but the iPhone XR has warmer tones which make the image look naturally attractive in the indoors.

The white balance on the iPhone XR camera is mostly accurate in all lighting conditions and does not show any odd colors even when shot with artificial sources of light such as the flash. In outdoor conditions, the white balance of the iPhone XR is a little more biased toward the colder blue tone whereas it remains on the warm side in indoor conditions, but remains very acceptable under both conditions.

Autofocus: 99

The autofocus on the iPhone XR is excellent as one would expect from high-end devices, which are equipped with Phase Detection Auto Focus (PDAF). Benchmark tests conducted under controlled lab environments showed that the iPhone XR was consistent in finding focus accurately and fast as well. During the test, the iPhone XR was exposed to defocusing between clicking images, keeping intervals of 500ms to 2000ms before requesting focus again and the iPhone XR surprised everyone as it still managed to focus and click sharp images and never failed to click a shot on autofocus. This procedure was repeated under a variety of lighting conditions and the results were consistent every time.

The zero shutter lag technology on the iPhone XR camera, which keeps buffering the frames while the camera app is on ensures that the camera clicks the exact same picture as you would see in the display at a given instance in time.

Texture: 75 Noise: 69

The iPhone XR features the same texture versus noise ratio as that of the iPhone XS Max. The recorded Accutane is over 80 percent when the camera is used in outdoor conditions, and the detail in still images is amazing. The details in static scenes remain very good even in low light conditions. The acutance is still recorded to be around 60 percent even in extreme low light conditions for static captures. If you are using a shutter speed of slower than 1/40 second in low light conditions of 20 lux or below, using the hand as well as the tripod will lead to a loss in detail in frames where there is a movement of the subject, where the acutance will be 1 lux for such images. You don't need to worry as this is acceptable behavior, and overall the iPhone XR does a wonderful job with its camera at capturing details.

Artifacts: 86

The iPhone XR scores low on artifacts for its flaws in image quality and optical deficiencies. The iPhone XR has the following areas of concern.

- Moiré effect in high-frequency patterns

- Ringing

- Flare in shots that have a backlight

- Minor color quantization

Ringing in the iPhone XR has been visible during high contrast edges in HDR shots. An example would be the visible railing in a bright sky. But if you are not printing the image out or viewing it on a large resolution, this can be neglected as it can be considered to be marginal to the overall quality of the image.

The moiré effect is a phenomenon that causes a rainbow appearing in your picture along the high-frequency areas of the shot where the resolution of your iPhone is not sufficient to capture fine details.

Flash: 83

The Flash on the iPhone XR gives better performance as compared to the iPhone XS Max since it provides better target exposure for faces and also in the center of the frame. We will not say that it is perfect as there is still evidence of flash only shots when the exposure is low but the algorithms on iPhone XR are definitely better than the iPhone XS Max for the Flash. You may see some vignette effects along the corner which are visible. The level of detail is good on Flash but there are some color quantization and residual noise, using both mixed lights and flash only shots. We can call it to be an improvement in the flash from the past iPhone models, but it is still not at par with a Google Pixel 2, which can be crowned as the king of Flash.

Zoom: 35

The image quality of the iPhone XR primary camera is as good as that of its elder siblings from the iPhone XS range. However, the single-camera setup on the iPhone XR fails to amaze for bokeh and zoom shots, where the dual camera setup of the iPhone XS and XS Max get an advantage. Using up to 2x zoom on the iPhone XR delivers images that are acceptable in both outdoor and indoor shots.

However, the difference between the single-camera setup and the dual camera setup becomes very visible when the zoom range is increased. If you increase the zoom range to 4x, you will notice that the iPhone XS Max preserves intricate details, such as the railings of a bridge. Although, the iPhone XR scores a little bit more in zoom detailing compared to the Google Pixel 2.

At medium range zoom of 4x and long-range zoom of 8x, the noise of the iPhone XR along with some artifacts like aliasing becomes very prevalent. Detail is still acceptable in bright conditions outdoors, and indoor shots to some extent as well, but do not expect to find fine details such as lines on brickwork or text on signboards when you are using the long-range zoom on your iPhone XR.

It is all right to admit that the iPhone XR's zoom is very limited compared to the iPhone XS or Google Pixel 2. Zooming to maximum magnification on the iPhone XR camera does not produce the same results like that on the iPhone XS or a Google Pixel 2. Nevertheless, for a single camera device, the iPhone XR gives a decent performance that is almost at par with the Google Pixel 2 but falls short of competing with the tele-lens zoom on the iPhone XS and XS Max.

Bokeh: 35

The quality of images in portrait mode also suffers a bit due to the absence of the tele-lens in the iPhone XR. The iPhone XR primary camera with its wide view comes with a 26mm lens, which is not exactly the best thing for portraits. You may try to get the subject into the frame by moving closer but you will observe that the facial features will undergo some distortion, anamorphosis, and especially on elements which are closer to the frame's edge.

The portrait mode in the iPhone XR works well on human subjects shot in low-light settings, resulting in getting better details on the face as compared to the iPhone XS, provided that the distance between the camera and the subject is less. Facial detail is perhaps the iPhone XR's best feature, and even though the bokeh effect helps separate the subject in the foreground from the background, we can't exactly call it perfect. The iPhone XR's camera in the absence of the tele-lens fails to calculate depth, resulting into the visibility of subject masking artifacts ultimately making the portrait look like a photoshopped cut-out where the subject was placed into the background.

The Bokeh test by DxOMark is for both still objects and humans.

As we have already discussed above, the iPhone XR's portrait mode works well with subjects with a face. The algorithm uses face detection, and therefore when used with still objects, the algorithm fails to trigger the bokeh effect leading to only the optical bokeh, which has very low efficiency. This is where the iPhone XR loses a few points to rival smartphones that are good with applying the bokeh effect to still objects as well. When the iPhone XR cannot detect a face in the frame while using the portrait mode, you will be prompted with a "no face detected" message.

Video Scores

DxOMark gives the iPhone XR and an excellent score of 96 points on Video because of its ability to capture beautifully in bright light environments. The final score is derived from a number of scores from the individual parameters such as:

- Color: 88

- Exposure: 88

- Autofocus: 92

- Noise: 77

- Texture: 57

- Stabilization: 94

- Artifacts: 84

The iPhone XR, overall, stands at par with the iPhone XS Max in terms of videography in outdoor videos with color rendering and the white balance being very good, and stabilization being excellent as well in slow motion. There are small instabilities with respect to exposure and white balance under inconsistent lighting scenarios. The level of detail is low on the iPhone XR when compared with the iPhone XS Max in low light conditions, but the noise is not much visible. This implies that Apple has worked its algorithm to strike a balance between noise and sharpness at a budget price.

The target exposure while capturing videos with an iPhone XR is very good in all possible lighting conditions down to 20 lux. The videos may come out dark when shot in extremely low light through 1 to 10 lux, but they are still pretty usable. Change in exposure while shooting in changing light is also good, with the transition time being negligible.

The white balance and color rendering work well through both indoor and outdoor conditions, and the level of saturation might go in low light, but it stays more than acceptable even in low light conditions.

The iPhone XR also impresses with texture preservation again through both indoor and outdoor videos. Although the texture suffers in low light, the noise to detail ratio is well managed. The iPhone XR preserves text and edges higher in indoor videos at 100 lux and even better in outdoor videos between 300 to 1000 lux.

The iPhone XR's autofocus works like a charm with videos just like it does with still pictures. This is because the iPhone XR is well balanced bundled with good response time and does not have any instabilities, jerkiness or overshoots that would disrupt the experience. The auto-focus works well in bright-light outdoor videos and the smoothness and tracking of the autofocus work efficiently too. The experience does not turn out to be as good in low-light environments but is still decent enough. The stabilization is consistent in all lighting conditions, frame sharpness is impressive and the videos tend to stay stable even when light conditions change. Motions related to panning and walking are controlled nicely too.

Best Single-lens Phone

The iPhone XR will be easily the most desired model of iPhones for Apple patrons who wish to upgrade their iPhones, given the rocketing price of the iPhone XS series launched a month before it. The single-cam implementation on the iPhone XR is what makes it very affordable, but this also means that you will have to compromise on some better features which are only bundled with the dual-cam XS series such as zoom and bokeh functions.

Apple has comfortably integrated the same software and image processing algorithms as that available in the iPhone XS series, and therefore the iPhone XR is at par with the functional capabilities of the iPhone XS and iPhone XS Max in many ways - - amazing exposure under all lighting conditions and an even better noise to detail ratio. The autofocus function also works well in all conditions.

The one place where the iPhone XR fails compared to its siblings in the X series is where the additions of a second camera with an extra sensor bundled with a tele-lens comes into the picture. So it would be naive to expect the same quality on zoom and bokeh effects The Portrait mode also looks a little bit artificial compared to the smooth portrait on the iPhone XS and XS Max.

The iPhone XR however, due to its better results for noise artifacts, take a spot over the Google Pixel 2 and becomes the best single-cam smartphone in the market.

Pros and Cons of the iPhone XR Camera

Pros

- Provides a dynamic range on exposure in indoor and bright light conditions

- Preserves detail well in all lighting conditions

- Colors achieved are vivid and pleasant

- Autofocus is accurate and fast

- Optimized image stabilization

Cons

- Detail preservation is low in medium to long range zoom shots

- Noise and fine grain luminance is visible in low-light shots

- Bokeh mode is not realistic

- Instability of white balance while indoors

The iPhone XR camera is bang for the buck. The software and image processing offers the same camera experience as that provided by the iPhone XS and XS Max, with the biggest and only difference being the telephoto lens on the iPhone XS series. Apple has shown its strengths through the amazing camera experience, which has been very consistent among all the smartphones of the current generation. It also provides a leading quality in pictures that stands at par with all the competition in the market. The iPhone XR performs well on low-light and although it does not match the picture quality of its elder siblings with the dual-cam setup, it still manages to leave the Google Pixel 2 behind it in terms of camera and picture quality in the single-cam setup.

Chapter 15: The Power of iOS 12

One of the things you will love about the iPhone XR is iOS 12. This revamped upgrade gives you one of the best iPhone experiences to date. You are looking at an iPhone that performs faster than most, is delightful, and more responsive. Everyone loves a responsive device. The iOS 12 has been dubbed one of the most advanced operating systems on mobile devices yet.

What Makes it Stand Out?

Regarding performance, the iOS 12 is designed to help you speed things up. Everything you have been using your iPhone for in the past, you can now do the same, at insane speeds. Take swiping your camera, for example, whose response has been improved by 70%.

You are also looking at a 50% improvement in the keyboard display speed, and if you are using your iPhone under a heavy workload, you will be able to launch apps up to two times faster than before.

The performance enhancements are some of the reasons why you are going to enjoy using the iOS 12 on your iPhone XR. Other minor enhancements go towards giving you an overall amazing experience on the iPhone XR.

Fancy some FaceTime with friends and family members? You can now interact with up to 32 people at the same time. The audio and video enhancements on the iPhone XR powered by the iOS 12 make this a lot easier. In a group setting, if someone is speaking, their tile is enlarged, allowing you to stay focused on the conversation.

iOS 12.1.1

When Apple released iOS 12.1.1, one group of users who had a lot to look forward to was iPhone XR users. With the update, you can now enjoy some of the Haptic Feedback features that were not present previously. This adds functionality to the device, especially when you use a long press to get more out of your notifications.

The updates released thus far are small, but allow you to enjoy utmost utility out of your iPhone XR. It has not been a smooth sailing experience for everyone, however. Soon after the upgrade, there have been issues with some users experiencing trouble connecting to their cellular networks. It is not a widespread concern, because the frequency of reports to this problem is random.

Other users have also reported enjoying full cellular use on their iPhone XR devices with select apps, but not all the apps. What this alludes to is that the device can identify and pick up the connection to a cellular signal, but the operating system is struggling to manage the connection.

This update includes support for third-party navigation assistance apps instead of having to depend on Apple Maps all the time. You can look forward to using Google Maps, for example, in CarPlay for iOS 12. However, you must update to the current release. Google Maps is popular for accurate information in terms of traffic information, finding places, and alternative routes. The fact that you can enjoy it in the in-built display on your device is a plus.

Assuming that you started getting directions on your iPhone XR and then you got into your car, you simply need to connect to CarPlay and Google Maps will continue from where you left on the phone.

If you are planning your commute between your home and the workplace, Google Maps will provide you live updates on traffic so you can plan your route efficiently. You also get access to some of the favorite spots you frequent, which is a good way to remind you to pick up something you might have forgotten.

Another important feature that you will enjoy with the iOS 12.1.1 upgrade on your iPhone XR is dual SIM support. This is a feature that iPhones have barely taken seriously over the years. However, the update enables an eSIM that comes built into the iPhone XR, iPhone XS, and iPhone XS Max. Instead of getting a second physical SIM card, you can simply activate your cellular plan on a different network.

Chapter 16: Setting Up Your iPhone XR

Once you get your hands on your new iPhone XR, you are probably excited about firing it up and enjoying what it has to offer. Here are some features that will get you buzzing right away:

Face ID – allows you to confirm mobile payments and unlock your phone with ease, so setting this up right away will be a good idea.

Because the traditional physical home button no longer exists on the iPhone XR, you will want to learn how to do simple things like closing apps, taking screenshots, turning off the device and switching between the apps you are using.

Once you have the device out of the box, you can set it up in the following ways:

- As a new device, a fresh installation without restoring any old settings from previous phones.

- Restore old photos, music, apps, and anything else from a cloud backup or a backup in your iTunes account.

- Restore data from an Android device.

Backup of the Old iPhone

If you own an iPhone already, there's a checklist of things you will need to create before you switch to the new iPhone XR. This chapter will help you transition as smoothly as possible from your current iPhone to your new iPhone XR.

Consider the following checklist during your move from your old iPhone to the new one.

This is a very important step while you migrate from your old iPhone to the new iPhone XR. You need to ensure that you have backed up all necessary data in the correct manner so that it becomes easy to later transfer it onto your new iPhone.

The easiest method to achieve this backup is by using iCloud.

You will need to navigate to Settings>>Apple ID>>iCloud and then use the toggle buttons and toggle everything you need to be backed up to "on."

Now scroll down to the iCloud Backup option and tap on "Back Up Now."

You may realize now that you need more space and this would be a good time to purchase a new iCloud storage plan. To do so, tap back and get into the iCloud settings, scroll to the top and get into Manage Storage. You can check your storage tier option here and purchase a plan accordingly.

Voilà! That is it and you are ready with your data backup. You can restore all this data onto your new iPhone XR while setting it up on first boot.

iTunes Backup

Power on the device and select your country and language. Your iPhone XR will prompt you to either restore settings from a backup, move data from your old Android device, or to set up your iPhone XR as a new phone.

Choose "Restore from an iTunes backup."

Use the provided Lightning to USB cable that comes with your device and connect it to your computer. In case your MacBook only has USB Type C ports, you must buy the Lightning to USB Type C cable.

If iTunes does not open automatically, open it, and you will be asked to allow the computer to access iPhone settings and information. Your iPhone will prompt you to accept whether you trust the connected computer.

On your iPhone, tap Trust, and on your computer, click Continue.

You will get a greeting message on the iPhone. Click Continue and Get Started.

Choose your iPhone on the list of devices that you can see on the left panel. Click on the iPhone summary tab. This tab should provide information on the type of device you are using, and useful information about the backups you have.

Select Restore Backup. In case you had saved backups for different devices, you can look at the time stamp to determine which of the backups is the most recent.

After restoring the backup, sync the iPhone XR to your computer, and then eject the drive.

iCloud Backup

Power on your iPhone XR and choose your country and language. You will be asked to choose how you want to set up the device, either from an Android device, as a new iPhone, or to restore settings and data from a backup.

Choose iCloud backup.

Enter the login details for your Apple ID account.

If you have turned on two-factor authentication, you should get an alert on any of your devices that are running iOS 10 or advanced models, or your MacBook, if it is running macOS Sierra or advanced models like macOS High Sierra and macOS Mojave.

Enter the code provided on your iPhone. Read and agree to the terms and conditions.

Look through the iCloud backups that you have, and going by the time stamp, choose the most recent.

Once you have selected the desired backup, decide whether you want to customize your settings on your new iPhone XR, or if you want to replicate the same settings you had on the old iPhone.

Your iPhone XR will then restore settings from the chosen iCloud backup.

Remember that this process might take a while, depending on how strong your Internet connection is. You can step away for a cup of coffee while you wait.

Chapter 17: The First Boot

Let's get you through the first boot on your new iPhone XR. You will be greeted with the Apple logo followed by a sweet Hello when you boot up the phone for the first time. You can then select your preferred language followed by your country or region. This will set up the language of your new iPhone over a few seconds.

You will then be directed to the "Quick Start" screen from where you start setting up your customizations on the iPhone. Tap on "Set Up Manually."

Naturally, the first thing the iPhone will ask you to do is set up and connect to your Home Wi-Fi network. Once you have set up the Wi-Fi on your iPhone, it may take a few minutes for the phone to be ready. Next, continue to accept Apple's Data and Privacy Policy and we then move on to set up your Face ID. Fix your face in the frame of the camera and move your face in different angles to complete setting up your Face ID. If you choose to set up the Face ID later, you will be prompted to keep a passcode instead. The phone will then continue setting up your Apple ID followed by these configurations.

Automatic Updates: You can click on continue to configure Automatic Updates or you can click on "Install Updates Manually."

Location Services: Click on "Enable Location Services" as this will switch on the GPS services and help with day-to-day applications like Uber and Maps.

Apple Pay: If you have your Credit Card handy, you can set up your Apple Pay details for purchases.

iCloud Keychain: Your password management system, which can be enabled with the help of another Apple device.

Siri: Set up Siri, your AI-powered personal assistant who is at your service to help you with all your needs.

Screen Time: Manage your time on the screen better by setting up Screen Time, which will give you weekly reports of time you spend on the phone. It will also allow you to set screen time limits for apps you want to cut down on.

iPhone Analytics: You can choose to share or not share statistics of your iPhone usage with Apple.

True Tone Display: A feature that lets the iPhone adjust to the light of its current environment such that colors appear to be consistent to you.

Display Zoom: Customize the kind of view you would like on your new iPhone XR using the options in this feature.

That is it and your iPhone is ready to use!

New Gestures

If you are upgrading from the iPhone X, you will already be familiar with most of the gestures on the iPhone XR as well. However, if you are coming from an iPhone 8 model or before, the following gestures and commands will help you ease your way into your new iPhone XR.

Notification Center: You can get to the Notification Center by swiping down from the top of the screen.

Home Screen: Swiping up on the home bar will land you on the home screen of your iPhone XR.

Control Center: Swiping down from the top right of the screen will get you to the Control Center.

Switching between Apps: If you want to switch between different open apps on the phone, you will need to swipe up and continue the swipe by performing a curved motion towards the right of the screen.

Siri: Swiping down from the center of the screen will activate your assistant to help you with your needs or even if you are in the mood to just hear a joke.

Reachability: Reachability is an iPhone feature introduced since iPhone 6 to shrink the screen size to smaller than the actual physical size of the display so that people with smaller hands can easily move their finger across the screen. Swiping down from just above the home bar will help you activate this feature.

Accessibility: The Accessibility feature in the iPhone allows you to set up voice commands for people who have challenges with respect to their vision. You can find the accessibility feature by triple tapping the side button.

Power-Off/SOS: Pressing and holding down the volume buttons simultaneously along with the power button will get you to the SOS mode.

Screenshot: To take a quick screenshot of your current screen, press the power button simultaneously along with the volume down button.

High-Efficiency Formats on your iPhone XR

Apple devices are equipped with software that is excellent with image compression and enabling this has a lot of benefits for your iPhone's camera.

Enabling this leads to almost 50 percent compression in size of the photos and videos while still retaining their high quality.

You can set this up by navigating to

Settings>>Camera>>Formats>>High Efficiency.

This is a must-have for anyone who is into clicking a lot of pictures and videos.

Setting up Safari Autofill and Face ID

We already spoke about the first boot up of your iPhone XR where you get to set up your Face ID. If you skipped that to be set up later, this is how you can set it up.

Navigate to

Settings>>Face ID and Passcode>>Set up Face ID.

You will have to face the camera and position your face in the circle on the screen, which resembles a head. You will then have to move your face in different angles such that maximum parts are registered. Your phone will confirm when the process is complete.

Once the Face ID is set up, you can proceed to select which apps and feature you want to be secured by Face ID. It is advisable to select everything including Password Autofill.

You also get the choice to set up an alternate appearance for yourself. This feature helps to make the facial recognition system versatile. So if you wear glasses, you can set up a facial ID with the glasses on, or it can actually be used to set up facial recognition for another person who you'd like to have access to the same phone.

You can turn off this feature known as attention awareness, which needs you to look at the screen before unlocking it. Switching it off will speed up the process of Face ID authentication but will add another step of security.

Setting up Safari Autofill is simple and you just need to ensure that iCloud Keychain is on in your iCloud settings.

Navigate to

Settings>>Passwords and Accounts>>Switch Autofill Passwords to enable.

Now go to Safari settings and select Autofill. Here, you can select your information, and enable the contact info Autofill.

You can also enter your credit card details to be used for payment pages.

You can now surf the web pages on the Internet on Safari and when you fill any information in forms, you will be prompted to save the information in Keychain. The iOS 12 upgrade also allows users to integrate third-party application like 1Password and Dashlane to manage their passwords.

Display Settings Customization

One of the things you need to do when you get your new iPhone XR is to set up the display so that you have a good experience with the colors.

Navigate to

Settings>>Display and Brightness.

Here, you will be able to customize the way your iPhone's display reacts to different environments.

1. Disable "Raise to Wake" if you don't want the screen to come on automatically when you raise your phone.

2. You can also change the auto-lock period to something other than the default 30 seconds.

3. You can use the "Night Shift" feature to schedule and customize your phone usage in the night so that it doesn't keep you up at night.

4. You can disable "True Tone" which is a feature that turns the screen in a paper-white tone in any lighting environment.

You can also enable or disable the Auto Brightness feature from

Settings>>General>>Accessibility>>Display Accommodations.

Control Center Customization

The Control Center on your new iPhone XR will look pretty bland and empty since there's not much that has been added to it.

Navigate to

Settings>>Control Center>>Customize Controls.

Here, you can add or remove controls for Notes, Apple TV Remote, Screen Recording, etc.

To add features, tap the green "+" sign to add them. You can remove them by tapping the red "-" sign and can arrange them by pressing on them and dragging them.

Protecting Your New iPhone XR

Lastly, we would advise you to purchase AppleCare+. If not, we suggest that you get a good screen protector and cover.

AppleCare+ has made a number of changes to its policies and you have up to 60 days after your iPhone purchase to decide whether you want AppleCare or not.

You can find many screen protectors and cases for your iPhone on Amazon for reasonable costs. However, if you are looking to purchase the best one, we recommend going for the ones directly provided by Apple.

Chapter 18: Network and Connectivity

Selecting a Network

You get 2 options when you insert a SIM in your iPhone XR. Either you can let it choose a network automatically or you can select a manual network for it.

Navigate to

Settings>>Mobile Data>>Mobile Network.

1. Automatic>>Toggle it to be On or Off.

2. If you are keeping it off, proceed further by selecting your desired network manually.

Press Mobile Data to save the setting.

Selecting a Network Mode

This option basically lets you decide which network modes your iPhone XR is allowed to use. Depending on that, your phone will achieve Internet speeds respectively.

Navigate to

Settings>>Mobile Data>>Mobile Data Options>>Enable 4G.

1. Off

2. Voice and Data

3. Data only

The 4G network can be used for voice calls through the mobile network, which results in a better and faster connection. If you deactivate 4G, your iPhone will automatically connect to 3G or 2G depending on availability.

Data on the 4G network is faster than that of 3G or 2G as well. An ideal 4G network can handle download speeds between 5 to 12 Mbps, upload speeds up to 5 Mbps, and can reach peak download speeds up to 50 Mbps.

Connecting to WLAN (Wi-Fi or Wireless network)

WLAN can be used as an alternative to using the mobile network when you want to connect to the Internet. When you're connected to the Internet using WLAN, your iPhone XR won't make use of mobile data.

Navigate to Settings>>Press Wi-Fi>>Toggle Wi-Fi to On.

A list of available Wi-Fi networks will be displayed. Select the network you are familiar with and key in the password to connect to the Wi-Fi Network.

Activate/Deactivate Mobile Data

You can limit the use of mobile data by deactivating it when it's not absolutely essential. This would ensure no connectivity to the Internet via the mobile network. You can still connect to the Internet using WLAN when the mobile data is deactivated.

Navigate to

Settings>>Mobile Data>>Toggle Mobile Data to On/Off.

Alternatively, if you want to restrict only particular apps from using mobile data, you could do so by scrolling down and toggling mobile data off for the required app.

Activate/Deactivate Data Roaming

When you are traveling outside your country of residence, the network provider who you have purchased the SIM from might not be offering services in the country you are traveling to. In such cases, your phone automatically latches on to an available network, which is known as Roaming. Similarly, roaming can get applied to your Data as well but it will cost you a lot of money if your plan does not support international roaming at reasonable costs. Thus it is always a wise choice to turn off data roaming while you are traveling. You can still always connect to an available WLAN network while you are in another country.

To turn off Data Roaming, navigate to

Settings>>Mobile Data>>Mobile Data options>>Data Roaming>>Toggle it to Off.

Using your iPhone XR as your Personal Hotspot

When you use your phone as a Personal Hotspot, you can use your phone's Internet connection to be shared wirelessly (WLAN) among other devices such as another phone or a laptop.

To set up a hotspot on your iPhone XR, navigate to

Settings>>Personal Hotspot>>Toggle it to On.

Set up a password of your choice to allow access to only people you want to give access to.

There are 3 options through which other devices can connect to your Hotspot.

1. Using Wi-Fi

2. Using Bluetooth

3. Using USB

Click on Done and you have set up your Personal Hotspot.

Activate/Deactivate GPS

Your iPhone XR can determine your location geographically by using the GPS (Global Positioning System). This information about your location is used by numerous apps on your iPhone such as Maps, Uber, etc.

To turn GPS off, navigate to

Settings>>Privacy>>Location Services>>Toggle it to Off.

If you leave it on, you also get options to manage GPS specifically for individual apps as well.

Chapter 19: iPhone XR Benchmarks

When the iPhone XS and iPhone XS Max were launched in September 2018, they met the expectation of the masses: they were not only the most performing iPhones ever made, but they were the fastest smartphones in the world. The A12 Bionic chip by Apple had crushed every other processor ever manufactured for a smartphone.

The iPhone XR is available with the A12 Bionic chip pumping its veins with the same adrenaline and is expected to deliver the same high-powered performance as its siblings. Also, given that the iPhone XR is big on battery life and low on resolution, which is 1792 x 828 pixels, it is expected to have a battery life, which lasts longer than any other iPhone in the market.

So if you live in a world where you only care about benchmarks, you simply need to get the cheapest iPhone of 2018. Let's see where the most popular benchmark tests place the iPhone XR in comparison to its sibling from the iPhone X family.

Geekbench 4

Geekbench is preferred by most techies for benchmarking devices because of its cross-platform availability for platforms such as Windows, iOS, Linux and Android. There is no benchmark test available in the market that can be called the perfect one across platforms but Geekbench 4 is the closest we can get.

The Geekbench 4 benchmark produced the following results for iPhone XR when compared with the iPhone XS and XS Max.

Compute Metal Performance

- iPhone XR: 22025

- iPhone XS: 21574

- iPhone XS Max: 21967

- iPhone X: 15691

CPU - Multi Core

- iPhone XR: 11326

- iPhone XS: 11382

- iPhone XS Max: 11096

- iPhone X: 10377

CPU - Single Core

- iPhone XR: 4818

- iPhone XS: 4807

- iPhone XS Max: 4813

- iPhone X: 4253

As we can see from the score, the iPhone XR is at par with the XS and XS Max with just a high or low of a few percentage points.

If we look at the single-core performance, it is 13 percent faster than iPhone X and about 10 percent faster in multi-core performance.

The performance of the iPhone XR also stands at 40 percent better than the iPhone X in the GPU powered compute metal test.

AnTuTu V7

Known for its popularity in the world of Android smartphones, AnTuTu is also available on iOS. The test produced different and varying results on every run when tried on the latest version of AnTuTu. So, it's not necessary to stress on these numbers but here are the results to satisfy everyone's curiosity.

GPU

- iPhone XR: 142593

- iPhone XS: 103170

- iPhone XS Max: 117224

- iPhone X: 20148

CPU

- iPhone XR: 120183

- iPhone XS: 115313

- iPhone XS Max: 121849

- iPhone X:103221

Overall

- iPhone XR:335174

- iPhone XS:305409

- iPhone XS Max: 309188

- iPhone X: 244204

It is surprising that the iPhone XR score more than the XS and XS Max in the GPU test, thus boosting its overall score. The reason for this is probably the low-resolution scheme on the iPhone XR display. The tests are rendered and performed on-screen and a fixed or off-screen resolution is avoided. The A12 Bionic chip delivers faster frames on the iPhone XR because the number of pixels to be rendered on iPhone XS and iPhone XS Max are 85 percent and 125 percent more respectively.

3DMark

3DMark is the favorite test for determining the graphics performance of everyone in the tech world.

There is a Slingshot version of the 3DMark test that runs a graphic intensive test, which is almost like a real game. It then delivers the test results based on the performance.

Sling Shot Extreme

- iPhone XR: 3602

- iPhone XS: 3557

- iPhone XS Max: 3595

- iPhone X: 3568

Sling Shot Extreme Unlimited

- iPhone XR: 4297

- iPhone XS: 3955

- iPhone XS Max:4067

- iPhone X: 3925

Given that the 3DMark test runs at a fixed resolution, the iPhone XR delivers almost the same performance as that of an iPhone XS and an iPhone XS Max.

The test is run on two different versions.

1. Sling Shot Extreme runs the test using the Metal API provided by Apple which starts at a resolution of 2560 x 1440 but is later scaled higher or lower as per the resolution of the device it is being tested on.
2. Sling Shot Extreme Unlimited performs the same test off-screen.

Note: neither of the tests is affected by the lower resolution of the iPhone XR.

The results of the iPhone XR are at par with that of the XS or XS Max, and also almost identical to that of the iPhone X. Apple had claimed that the A12 Bionic chip will up the graphics performance by 50 percent; however, this is not the case as seen from the results where the iPhone X is at par with the XR, XS, and XS Max. We believe this has happened because the test is also largely dependent on the memory and cache performance of the device over just the GPU performance.

We, therefore, do a simple Ice Storm test to see if it proves our theory. This test runs a simple scene like a game by implementing OpenGL ES 2.0 through a fixed resolution of 1280 x 720 resulting in all devices rendering the exact same frames.

CPU - Multi-Core

- iPhone XR: 77344

- iPhone XS: 75528

- iPhone XS Max: 77022

- iPhone X: 64382

As this test is less stressful on the processor, it demands less memory and cache. Therefore as seen from the results, it runs 18 percent faster on an A12 chip compared to that on an A11 chip.

Chapter 20: iPhone XR Tips and Tricks

The iPhone XR is a unique device in the line of iPhone products. Retailing below $1,000, it is the first device that has Face ID and an edge-to-edge design. This is a device that is simply designed for use by everyone. Whether you are upgrading from an iPhone 6 or an iPhone 8, this is the device you should run to.

There is a lot that you can learn to help you get the utmost utility from this device. It might take you a while to get used to the tweaks, but once you do, this will be one of the best mobile experiences you have had in years. The following are some useful tips that will help you make the most use of your phone.

Waking your Phone Up

Unlike the previous devices, iPhone XR has a Tap to Wake feature. If you do not want to fiddle with the side button, tap on the screen and it will wake up. This is ideal if you want to check notifications and get back to whatever you were doing.

Accessing Home

The Home button is conspicuously missing in the iPhone XR. To access Home, swipe up on your screen from the bottom. This gesture will also unlock your iPhone XR.

App Switcher

To access App Switcher, swipe up from your Home bar, but hold on briefly. However, for an on-the-go user, this is a waste of time. Instead of doing this, swipe up on your screen from the left edge at 45 degrees. This gets you to the App Switcher.

Accessing the Notification Center

To view your notifications from the notification center, swipe down from the notch area.

Accessing Control Center

Swipe down from either the right ear or right edge close to the notch to access the Control Center. From here, you can customize settings as you please to include settings for Accessibility, your Apple TV remote, and so forth.

Making Payments

Using Apple Pay for payments is very easy. Press your side button twice – it is on the right side of the phone. Hold your iPhone XR to your face and use Face ID to scan your face.

Switching between Recent Apps

The iPhone XR comes with a Quick App switcher gesture. With this, you can switch between your recent apps seamlessly. To access an app you used previously, swipe right. Keep swiping to access the apps further. A left swipe takes you back to the app you accessed first.

This only works if you do not interact with any app. If you do, the system detects this, and you have to swipe right to access the one you were using previously. This is a simple process, but it can be confusing. You will need some practice to familiarize yourself with it.

Taking Screenshots

You do not have a Home button on the iPhone XR, so taking a screenshot the traditional way is not possible. For screenshots, press and hold the volume down button and the lock button.

Using Siri

The easiest way to access Siri is to press and hold the lock button. Alternatively, if you are not comfortable with this setting, you can set up Hey Siri for additional functionality.

Rebooting your device

The lack of a home button makes some mundane tasks on the iPhone seem complicated, like rebooting your phone. Hold the lock button and any of the volume buttons to reboot your device.

Perform a hard reset

There is nothing special about a hard reset. It is but an elevated reboot. In case you were wondering, a hard reset does not erase data from your phone. Press volume up, volume down, then press and hold the hold button until the Apple logo appears on your screen.

Creating Memojis

Emojis have been delightful highlights to many conversations. With the Face ID and the TrueDepth camera on the iPhone XR, you get to animate your emojis and make conversations more entertaining. The Memoji is an advanced form of emoji that is more fun to work with. When using a Memoji, you are creating a Bitmoji-like character on your phone. To create a Memoji, go to Messages, choose any iMessage chat and click on the Animoji app, then proceed.

Depth Effect Selfies

Having an iPhone with an amazing camera sensor is a good thing. You are able to take amazing selfies with depth effect. On your camera, change to portrait mode and flip your iPhone XR for this unique selfie.

Managing Notifications from your Lock Screen

The iOS 12 brings advanced user abilities to the iPhone XR. From your lock screen, you can access and manage notifications. To do this, swipe left on any notification notice and tap Manage.

This is where you can turn off notifications for apps that you do not need to receive frequently. Other settings include Deliver Quietly, where the app does not show notifications on your lock screen. Your phone will not make a sound if the app has any notifications. However, to access such notifications, you must open the Notification Center.

Two-Pane Landscape View

The two-pane landscape view is characteristic of the iPhone XS Max. Apple also introduced this in the iPhone XR. On your phone, perhaps you are accessing Mail, and you also need to keep track of some notes, just flip your phone to the side, and you will get the same two-pane view that you should be familiar with when using an iPad.

Face ID Fails

As amazing as Face ID is, at times it becomes a bother when it gets wonky. If you try to initiate Face ID and it fails, you can give it a second try. Do not enter your passcode just yet, instead, swipe up and you will get the settings right.

Multiple Face ID Faces

iOS 12 allows you to register more than one face for Face ID. Perhaps you need to share your phone with your partner, so this would come in handy. All you need to do is add a second face to your Face ID settings.

Go to Settings, select Face ID, then Set Up an Alternative Appearance. Your iPhone XR will give you prompts to follow, until you are done setting up a second face.

Bring back the Home Button

While some people have made peace with the fact that the Home Button is no more, others cannot move on that easily. If swipe gestures to enjoy Home Button services are not your thing, you can use the AssistiveTouch Home Button. This is a virtual feature that allows you to bring back the home button.

Go to Settings, then Accessibility, and select AssistiveTouch.

From here, you can create shortcuts for 3D Touch, long press, single tap, and double tap. You can define unique gestures for different responses.

Editing Depth from Portrait Shots

Your iPhone XR might only come with one camera, but this does not limit you from getting the most out of it. Having taken photos, you can still edit them later on with depth effect. In photo view, tap on edit and use the slider at the bottom of the screen to alter the depth effect as you desire.

Setting up Fast Charge

The iPhone XR comes with a 5W charger. For someone who uses their phone all the time, it will run out of juice. The iPhone XR supports a fast charge, so a fast charger will come in handy. If you have an iPad, you can use your 12W charger for your iPhone XR.

Taking RAW photos

The default iPhone camera is decent as it is. You can do so much with it, without any added settings. However, if you need full control of things like shutter speed, focus, and exposure, you must install a third-party application. One of the best for this is Halide, which allows you to take RAW photos.

Shortcuts for task automation

The iPhone XR is one of the smartest devices you will ever get in the market at the moment. Some tasks, especially repetitive ones, can be automated. You can also group others together. The

Shortcuts app helps you create shortcuts that can, among other things, send messages, read headlines, change the Do Not Disturb mode, turn off the lights and so forth, all with a single command.

Water Resistance

In a market that has a lot of phones that are capable of doing amazing things underwater, the iPhone XR is not one of them. This is an IP67 phone, which means that it is only splash resistant. Do not take it swimming. If it happens to drop in water, do not let it stay submerged for a long time. At the same time, resist the temptation to use your phone underwater.

Protection from theft and loss

You can lose your phone in different circumstances. With Apple Care+ Theft and Loss Protection, you do not need to worry about these anymore. It will cost you $249, but if you ever lose your iPhone XR, or if it is stolen, you can get a replacement. The good thing about this plan is that you can break it down in manageable installments.

Message Previews on your Lock Screen

How do you want to access your messages? Previews are a good thing. They help you brush through messages without having to lose time reading all of them. By default, your iPhone XR does not show message previews until you scan your face with Face ID. In terms of privacy, this is an awesome feature.

However, some people who need instant access to message previews feel this is too much. For those who prefer the screen waking up irrespective of the angle to access the notifications, using Face ID to preview messages can be a bother. You can disable this easily. Navigate to Settings, then Notifications, and select Show Previews, then choose Always.

Chapter 21: iPhone XR vs iPhone XS

A lot has been said about the iPhone XR, especially when pitting it against the iPhone XS. There are shared features and some dissimilarities here and there. Overall, however, these are two amazing phones. The release of the iPhone XR was marked by a lot of expectation, being that it was an exciting device, and at an affordable price.

Choosing between an iPhone and an Android device is often an easy choice because you are probably looking at the price, the brand you are loyal to, unique features, and so forth. However, if you have to choose between two or more iPhone devices, it can be quite a challenge. Price alone cannot be the deciding factor. You have to go deeper, learn more about the devices so that you make an informed decision. This comparison will pit the iPhone XR and iPhone XS.

Display

One of the first things you notice when comparing an iPhone XR and an iPhone XS is the display disparities. The iPhone XS has a smaller screen than the iPhone XR. Which one is better of the two?

Someone who fancies large screen devices will go for the iPhone XR. However, what are you getting in an iPhone XR that you cannot find in an iPhone XS, in light of the screen? Is a big screen always the better option in terms of experience and utility?

Experts contend that the iPhone XR screen is inferior to the iPhone XS. The iPhone XS has an OLED screen at 5.8 inches. The iPhone XR only has an LCD screen, at 6.1 inches.

Other than the dimensions according to size, you get True Tone 2436 x 1125 pixels at 458 ppi on the iPhone XS, compared to the True Tone 1792 x 828 pixels at 326 ppi on the iPhone XR.

The contrast ratio on the iPhone XS is 1,000,000:1 versus 1,400:1 on the iPhone XR. The screen to body ratio is 82.9% on the iPhone XS, compared to 79.0% on the iPhone XR.

Based on the display parameters, the iPhone XR is a downgrade from OLED to LCD, compromising on a few display comforts that most iPhone users are used to. The resolution on the iPhone XR is significantly lower. It gets so bad, and you cannot experience full HD content at 1080p on the iPhone XR. For a device that boasts of 6.1 inches of screen surface, this is a let-down. There are many devices in the market that offer far superior display parameters for a fraction of what Apple is charging.

iPhone XR

Since the introduction of iPhone 6S, 3D Touch technology has been a prominent feature in iPhones, which is surprisingly missing in the iPhone XR. However, Apple makes up for this by making it HDR10 and Dolby Vision compliant just like the iPhone XS. This is brilliant, especially since you are able to enjoy high-quality videos on the iPhone XR.

Looking at the OLED screens, an LCD screen might not be able to pack a punch, especially when you are looking at the black levels and contrast ratio. However, for many an average iPhone user, the LCD screen is more than sufficient.

Just in case you feel the 326 ppi is not sufficient, a kind reminder would suffice, that it was the same resolution depth that was used in the iconic iPhone 8. Besides, 326 ppi is more than what you would get in a 40" 4K TV, which only serves you 110 ppi. The aspect ratio on the iPhone XR is still the same as what you get on the iPhone XS, 19:5:9. The iPhone XR also gets a True Tone color accuracy, with 120Hz touch sensing, which allows you to enjoy a more responsive touch input.

iOS 12 brings forth a lot of advancements that make it easier for you to enjoy a variety of functions that would have been missing without 3D Touch. On the brighter side, however, there has been a slow uptake and appreciation of 3D Touch from users, and in response, Apple is shelving it altogether. In retrospect, the display is one of the biggest differences between the iPhone XR and the iPhone XS, though most people won't care.

Model design and finishes

When you look at the iPhone XR and iPhone XS, the two devices almost look similar. However, they are not. There is a very small difference between the two devices:

iPhone XR - 150.9 x 75.7 x 8.3 mm (5.94 x 2.98 x 0.33 in) and 194 g (6.84 oz)

iPhone XS - 143.6 x 70.9 x 7.7 mm (5.65 x 2.79 x 0.30 in) and 177g (6.24 oz)

As you can see, the iPhone XR is slightly larger than the iPhone XS, but this also means an additional 10% in weight. This is attributed to the weight of the LCD display screen. The LCD is traditionally less flexible compared to OLED displays, which means you cannot fit it comfortably into the iPhone chassis. This explains the presence of larger bezels on the sides of the iPhone XR.

The iPhone XS gets a premium feel thanks to the stainless steel chassis, making it a fancier option than the iPhone XR. The iPhone XR features a 7000 series aluminum chassis, the same model that was used in the iPhone 8 and the predecessor models. The iPhone XR only gets an IP67 water resistance rating, compared to the IP68 water resistance rating that is used in the iPhone XS.

The IP68 rating allows you to submerge the iPhone XS in water for no more than half an hour if the water depth is no more than two meters. These are simple features that most average users would not care about. On the bright side, while the iPhone XR has thicker bezels compared to the iPhone XS, they still come out thinner than most of the other OLED devices that are available in the market.

Both of the devices have external stereo speakers on the left and right, which deliver 25% louder sound than their predecessors. They also have dual SIM support, and you can use an internal eSIM or a nano SIM. Therefore, you can use both your home and travel sim on the same device. The good thing about this is that it is a feature that has never been present in any iPhone device since the beginning of time.

In terms of the appeal, iPhone XS comes limited to three colors (Gold, Space Grey, and Silver), while the iPhone XR is available in six colors (Coral, Yellow, Blue, Black, White, and Red). If you are the kind of user who appreciates diversity and something that gives you true perspective, the iPhone XR is your best bet. It has even been dubbed a more interesting model of the iPhones released in 2018.

Performance

One of the things that you will appreciate about the iPhone XR is the fact that it is running the same chipset that powers the iPhone XS. These two devices are all running Apple's A12 Bionic chipset. The chipset features a six-core CPU, four-core GPU, and an M12 motion coprocessor.

What sets them apart that the iPhone XS is loaded with 4 GB of memory, while the iPhone XR comes in a distant second with only 3 GB. Where will you feel this difference? Most people will barely notice. However, if you are someone who likes to multitask on their device, over time, you will notice a slight lag in performance.

It might not be apparent, especially when you are running light apps. However, if you are a gamer, or you use a lot of apps that are resource intensive, you will notice a difference. The reason why your apps will lag in performance is that you have a lot of them hogging your memory space, without allowing the device to reload.

The experts at Apple do contend, however, that there is a good reason why the iPhone XS was fitted with a larger RAM than the iPhone XR. The iPhone XS has two cameras. It needs additional memory resources to power the dual camera functions. If you want to know that 3 GB on the iPhone XR is not something to frown upon, take a step back and think about the iPhone X. This device was loaded with 3 GB of RAM, but you will not come across people complaining that it is a slow device.

Demystifying the A12 Bionic Chipset

What is so special about this chipset? The term bionic attached to the name is a pure marketing gimmick. However, that should not take away the important points about this chipset. Ideally, what you are getting through this chipset is a 50% improvement in power efficiency when your iPhone XR is running idle, or in terms of the graphics performance. Other than that, you will get an improvement in the CPU performance, of up to 15% based on the predecessor model.

There is a good reason why the A12 chipset is setting Apple, and all devices that are running it, a cut above the rest. In terms of competition, iPhone X, released in 2017 is considerably faster than any other Android device that was released in 2018. This means that Apple is just that good. They do not need the power, but they are giving it to you because they can.

Whether you are getting the iPhone XR or the iPhone XS, you will appreciate the power reserve capacity in the device. How important is this to you? Power reserves help you with NFC transactions. You should be able to complete the transactions even when your battery has run out. This is a feature that Apple has built into all the devices that were released in 2018, and hopefully will be a mainstay in the future, with a few improvements, of course.

Back in the day, iPhones were built incompatible with 600 MHz 4G bands. These bands are useful especially in areas where there was no signal. Apple has built this into the iPhone XR and the iPhone XS. This is a step in the right direction, opening up new frontiers for the tech giant.

However, even though the iPhone XR is able to support 4G, it is not fitted with the 4G Cat 16 LTE speed that is built into the iPhone XS. With this support, the iPhone XS can support downloads up to one gigabit. To be honest, this is too much power in one device. However, even without that, the iPhone XR still has a Cat 12 600 Mbit speed support, whose power is more than most average users need on their devices. There are credible reports that Apple might still be lagging behind in terms of adding 5G support to their devices. However, if you are getting such amazing speeds on your 4G enabled device, there is no reason for you to worry.

Cameras

Everything about the iPhone XR and the iPhone XS is the same when we consider optics, especially the dual rear camera. Other than the differences in display size, the only other feature that you can recognize almost immediately between these two is that the iPhone XR only has one rear camera. Let's take a closer look at the camera specifications of these two devices:

They both have a primary rear camera, 12MP, f/1.8 aperture, 1.4μm pixel size. The camera supports Optical Image stabilization (OIS), Quad-LED True Tone flash, and Portrait Lighting.

While the iPhone XR does not have a secondary rear camera, the iPhone XS has a secondary telephoto lens with the following features: 12MP, f/2.4 aperture, 1.0μm pixel size, OIS, and 2x optical zoom.

For the front camera, the two devices both have a TrueDepth camera, 7MP, and f/2.2 aperture.

Is it a good thing that the iPhone XR does not have 2x optical zoom on it? Some people would agree, others would be indecisive. However, how often do you need to zoom into an object to capture it? Most people just move closer to the object and take awesome shots. Bearing this in mind, you might not really miss it.

If we look at some of the earlier models, they all needed a secondary camera to help in taking good Portrait Mode shots. The iPhone XR, however, is capable of doing this with the rear and single front cameras, so you will do just fine with it.

One other thing that Apple has done on the iPhone XR and the iPhone XS is to offer HDR image processing. The beauty of HDR image processing is that you are able to combine lots of photos taken from unique exposure angles and combine them into one image. This feature was built into the devices to address an issue that Apple devices have always had since time immemorial, a weakness with dynamic range. With this in mind, the iPhone XR and iPhone XS can offer the same experience you would enjoy when you are using a Google Pixel 2, which has been dubbed one of the phones with the best cameras.

Both of the iPhones have an enlarged pixel size on the primary rear cameras. A larger pixel size makes them allow more light in, which is an important upgrade to improve photography in low light settings.

Charging and battery life

A lot of people often expect that they will get longer battery life on a more expensive device. This is not the case when you compare the iPhone XR and the iPhone XS. In terms of the battery life, we have to go back to the OLED and LCD comparison and learn something important. An LCD display does not consume as many resources as an OLED display.

The upside to using an LCD display on the iPhone XR over the OLED display used in the iPhone XS is that you are getting a lower resolution on the XR than the XS. A low resolution consumes less power, and since the phone comes in a larger size, Apple has enough room to load the device with a larger battery.

On the iPhone XR, you are getting 2,942 mAh, while the iPhone XS only offers 2,658 mAh. Why is this important? The iPhone XR, running this battery, is capable of lasting 25% longer than the iPhone XS on most functions. In fact, the iPhone XR can even outlast the iPhone XS Max, yet this was the flagship model.

However, there is a catch when it comes to the iPhone XR. It does not support fast wireless charging. Whether or not users will struggle to accept this, we will probably see in the next rollout of iPhone devices.

For wired charging, both the iPhone XR and iPhone XS are supported. If your device is flat out, you can get it up to 50% charging in half an hour. However, in traditional fashion, Apple still refuses to include a fast charger in the box when you buy the phone. You have to fork out an additional $75 to get the compatible cable and fast charger.

Cost consideration

If you need a wired fast charger for your devices, you will need to consider adding another $75 to your purchase price. However, that aside, the iPhone XR is still popular as the most affordable Apple device in its range.

This is how the devices compare: iPhone XS

- 64GB at $999

- 256GB at $1,149

- 512GB at $1,349

iPhone XR

- 64GB at $749

- 128GB at $799

- 256GB at $899

Final Note

A lot of brands are barely keeping up with iPhones when it comes to sales. Most of the iPhones are sold out in record time. What comes out clearly is that the iPhone XR is set to rival and probably threaten the flagships iPhone XS and iPhone XS Max in sales numbers.

Most of the features available in the iPhone XS have been maintained on the iPhone XR, with a few being hived off. While it is easy to complain about this on the face of it, a closer look would reveal that most of what has been scaled down to produce the iPhone XR are items that a lot of people can do without.

What might, perhaps, make a lot of people consider spending more to get the iPhone XS, is the OLED screen, bezel size, and dual camera. However, for most an average iPhone user, the iPhone XR is priced just right, and is a decent phone, by all means, possible, making it a worthy purchase.

If you look at the iPhone XR from a practical point of view, it is a device that is reasonable. Think about battery life, and for most people who love attention, it is available in a lot of color options. The iPhone XR remains one of the most amazing and exciting devices that Apple has released in a very long time.

Chapter 22: Software at a Glance

The iPhone XR comes with the iOS 12 on it and the software is a part of the iOS 12 bundle. We will run through it so that you know what to expect from an iPhone XR with respect to pre-loaded software.

The iPhone XR coupled with the iOS 12 has a new gesture system. We have already discussed the gesture system in detail in the chapter "First Things First."

Also, note that the iPhone XR does not come with 3D touch like its more expensive siblings, and therefore, the way you can experience a bit of it on the iPhone XR is by simply tapping and holding the screen. This keeps the iPhone XR far behind in the race from its siblings as 3D touch is only used when performing quick actions on the icons and these actions are swifter when you do the tap and hold action.

Let's take a ride through all the apps that come on the iPhone XR as a part of the iOS 12 bundle.

Facetime

Facetime is a proprietary application that was developed by Apple for video communication. Any iOS device equipped with a front facing camera and iOS version 10.6.6 or above supports Facetime. Apple also has an audio version of Facetime called Facetime Audio, which is supported by any Apple device running iOS 7 or higher. Facetime was introduced as a free app in iOS and MacOS from the Mac OS X Lion release.

Photo

All the pictures that you click with your iPhone and iPad are accessible through the Photos app. The app has evolved over the years and now supports editing and sharing features.

Mail

Mail, previously known as Apple mail, is the Email client that is available on Apple devices. It evolved from NeXTMail, which was developed by NeXT originally as a part of the NeXTSTEP OS.

You can configure an email account on mail using popular protocols such as SMTP, POP, and IMAP.

Mail app also supports pre-loaded configurations of popular Email providers such as Google, Yahoo, Hotmail, AOL, etc.

Clock

The clock app lets you set the time of your device. In addition to this, it also supports World time in case you have friends and family in different time zones.

Maps

Apple Maps is an application that is widely used by the traveling community while touring the world. It also comes handy on a daily routine basis for your commute between work and home as it helps you understand real-time traffic.

Weather

Apple Weather lets to pull weather details from the Apple database for any city, country, or region in the world.

Calendar

The calendar app lets you add entries to the calendar for any upcoming events and let's you plan out your day.

Notes

Notes is a simple app which lets you keep adding notes every now and then you come across something that you wish to jot down for a quick glance later.

Reminders

Reminders app lets you set up appointment reminders or any other reminder, which would show up as a prompt at the time that you have set it for.

Apple News

Why buy a newspaper when you have Apple News? The app gives you access to all the leading newspapers and numerous magazines online. You also get the option to go through past issues of a newspaper or magazine. Additionally, you can also download a magazine to be kept for reading at a later time.

Stocks

If you are a person who invests in the stock market, then stocks is the app you need. You can follow all the daily ups and downs in the stock market. You also get to customize a ticker such that it focuses on the companies that interest you. Business news from all top publications in the world is also included as a part of the stock app.

iTunes Store

It is the hub to listen to all kinds of music, videos, etc. The app adapts to your choices and suggests to you the kind of music you would like.

App Store

App Store is your one-stop destination for all the applications available for your iPhone. These include applications by Apple itself as well as new applications developed by 3rd party Apple application developers.

Books

You can access all the popular books available in the world and purchase them off the Apple Books app.

Home Kit

The Apple Home Kit app basically lets you connect to all Apple supported home devices such as lights, music systems, locks, etc.

Wallet

Apple Wallet is an alternative to carrying your physical credit cards with you everywhere. You can use your wallet to make payments at a number of merchants around the world.

Podcasts

If you are a person who loves listening to podcasts, the podcasts app will let you access all the popular podcasts from around the world at the tap of your finger.

Find My iPhone

Works with your GPS on your Apple phone to help you locate your iPhone in case you end up losing it or misplacing it.

Contacts

The Contacts app is where all your contact details are stored.

Files

The Files App provides you with a File Manager to perform actions on all the files available on your storage in your iPhone. You can move files from one folder to another and organize it in any way you wish.

Watch

The Apple watch on your iPhone lets you customize faces for your watch, configure notifications and settings, install apps on your physical watch, etc.

Voice Memos

Record audio clips on your iPhone and then edit it or share it. After you create a voice memo, you can easily replace a part of it, trim it or even delete a part of it.

Compass

The Compass is a handy app for the traveler in you. It shows you the direction to which your iPhone is pointing, the elevation, and your current location.

Measure

Through the integration of augmented reality, the measure app turns your iPhone into a measuring tape. You can measure the size of objects, detect dimensions of objects, and also save a picture of the measurement to be referred to later.

Calculator

A simple app to perform all the basic mathematical calculations.

Clips

The Clips app lets you create and share video clips by adding simple edits like text, graphics and more to them.

iMovie

iMovie is an application provided by Apple to edit videos. It was released in 1999 originally on Mac OS 8. Once a paid application, iMovie is now offered free of cost on the latest Apple devices.

iTunes U

The app was developed keeping students in mind. The iTunes U app lets you organize homework seamlessly and deliver assignments, lessons, and stay connected with your peers.

Apple TV

The Apple TV app lets you maintain your watchlist with your iPad, iPhone, and your Apple TV. The Apple TV app was initially only available in the USA but is now available in the UK as well.

Safari

The Safari app is the web browser provided on Apple device, which lets you surf the World Wide Web through a smooth experience.

Phone

The phone app is used to make phone calls to contacts in your iPhone.

Messages

The Messages app is used to send messages using the SMS

protocol.

Music

Apple Music is the music player app on your iPhone. It lets you add songs, create playlists, and even suggests songs based on your listening history. This is a subscription-based service.

Sheets

Sheets is Apple's alternative for Google Sheets and Microsoft Excel. If you are a person who likes to work on their worksheets while on the go, the Sheets app will make your life easy.

Pages

Pages is again Apple's alternative to Google Docs and Microsoft Word. It lets you create documents while on the go. It is particularly useful for writers and editors who like to note down things as and when they make a way to their mind.

Keynote

Keynote is Apple's alternative for Google Slides and Microsoft PowerPoint. It lets you create beautiful presentations on the go and is widely used by corporate professionals.

GarageBand

Apple provides a fully equipped virtual studio for creating music. This comes packed with a full-fledged sound library, which includes presets for the guitar and voice, instruments, and a variety of choices for drummers and percussionists. GarageBand has made it very easy to compose, edit, and share new musical compositions with everyone.

Conclusion

The iPhone XR's performance is at par with the iPhone XS series, which means you will be getting a top-notch experience.

The battery life is better than the iPhone XS series and this gives an advantage to the gamer's community as the GPU benefits highly from this and gives a better gaming experience compared to the iPhone XS and XS Max.

What makes the iPhone XR stand out? Even though it made headlines as one of the most affordable iPhones yet, you are still getting some fantastic features. You are getting a phone that is larger than an iPhone X and still offers the same unrivaled user experience. Apple decided to maintain the TrueDepth camera on the iPhone XR, having made a cameo on the iPhone X in 2017.

That aside, the Home button goes away, and so does the Touch ID. In place of the Home button and Touch ID, Apple is introducing TrueDepth camera and Face ID. Without a Home button, you must now swipe on the display from the bottom to get you back to the Home screen, a feature that was introduced with the iPhone X.

In terms of the design, a lot of things about the iPhone XR are a build off the back of iPhone X and iPhone XS. Looking back to the earlier designs, the new iPhone XR also has a similar glass and metal modern design concept which features curves around all corners. At the top, it also has a notch like the predecessors. What Apple has done with the iPhone XR is to continue in the reinvention that was aimed at marking a launch in the next frontier, the future 10 years of the iPhone.

There are notable differences between the iPhone XR and the predecessors. A quick glance will reveal the bezels have been made thicker around the display area. The screen to casing ratio has reduced to give users a complete full-screen effect when using the iPhone XR. However, these are differences that you would barely notice if you were not holding the iPhone XR and a close comparison hand to hand. If you take the comparison further to an iPhone 8, you will notice wholesale differences.

Given the features available on the iPhone XR, who would be the ideal target for it? Well, in case you have an iPhone 8 or any of the older iPhones, you might want to consider getting an iPhone XR.

We finally find ourselves coming to the final paragraph of this little book on the iPhone XR. It is clear that when the iPhone XS series was out, we all agreed that the price being asked by Apple is a tad too much. But with the release of the iPhone XR, Apple has finally played a masterstroke in the smartphone market.

In the end, the final and big question is if the iPhone XR is value for your money with everything that it has to offer and a few things that it lacks in comparison to its more expensive siblings. Well as for the cost, it is definitely the most worthy iPhone that has ever come to the market. The point to be noted is that Apple has not compromised on technology to make the iPhone XR affordable as it is equipped with the latest A12 Bionic processor. All this kept in mind, the iPhone XR definitely provides better value in comparison to the iPhone XS alternatives.

43643980R00073

Made in the USA
Middletown, DE
26 April 2019

WHORE

MATT SHAW

WARNING
The following book contains scenes and descriptions which some people may find
upsetting. Please be aware this is an extreme novel intended for a mature audience.
***

www.facebook.com/mattshawpublications

www.mattshawpublications.co.uk